# KEY TO THE COVER ART

Pure Spirit

Primordial Cause

Intellect

Ego

Mind

5 Potentials
5 Cognitive Senses
5 Active Organs
5 Elements

Śiva (You) in Absorption / Union

# THE SPIRITUAL FOUNDATION OF YOGA

## Understanding Nature & Spirit

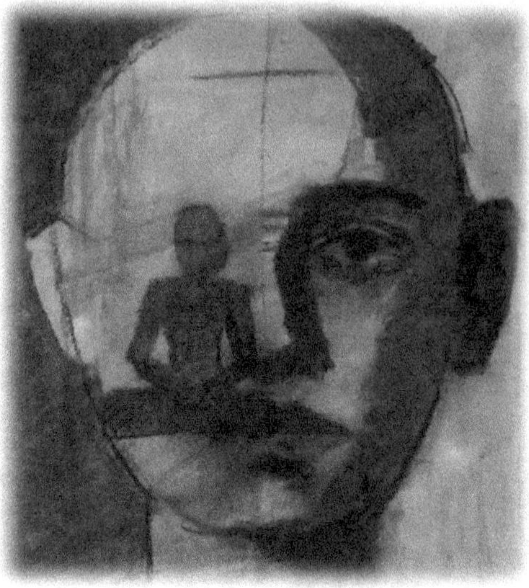

# THE SPIRITUAL FOUNDATION OF YOGA

## Understanding Nature & Spirit

Suraj Sarode

Quintessence

**THE SPRITUAL FOUNDATION OF YOGA**

by Suraj Sarode



**Hardcover ISBN**: 979-8-9880622-4-0
**Paperback ISBN**: 979-8-9880622-5-7
**eBook ISBN**: 979-8-9880622-6-4

Cover art and design by Michele Maselli
Sanskrit to English translation by Suraj Sarode
Content editing by Tracey Cook
Proof reading by Dorus de Vries

Publication assistance and digital printing in the United States, Canada, the UK, Australia, the EU, and Brazil by Lightning Source®

Print editions distributed worldwide by Ingram
Ebook edition distributed online by Google Play Books

"The meditative state is called always the highest state by the *Yogi*, when it is neither a passive nor an active state; in it, you approach nearest to the Puruṣa.

The soul has neither pleasure nor pain;
it is the witness of everything,
the eternal witness of all work,
but it takes no fruits from any work.

... the soul is neither passive nor active, it is beyond both. The nearest way of expressing this state of the soul is that it is meditation. This is Sāṅkhya philosophy."

— Swami Vivekananda

# DEDICATION

I dedicate this book to my primary teacher of Sanskrit. He offered his teaching openly and freely, never asking anything in return. Others and I studied with him for years in Varanasi. Strangely, he never told us his name, and we never bothered to ask.

In addition, I would also like to dedicate this book to every student of Yoga searching for deeper meaning and a spiritual basis for his or her practice – a practice that is only possible due to Yoga's development from the root philosophy of Sāṅkhya.

This book is for you.

# CONTENTS

# FOREWORD

I met Suraj-ji for the first time in Rishikesh when he was doing research work on Soma with Erik-ji. I was at the time studying and sharing Yogic practices, the Yogic classical text Yoga Sutras, and Hatha Yoga texts to those who were interested in Yoga practices. It was great to meet and to know him, and listen to stories of his spiritual journey. His deep fire within took him to different expert teachers of the subject, dedicated study of Sanskrit grammar (vyākaraṇa), the Upaniṣads, Indian spiritual philosophy (bhāratīya dharma) and his unique approach to presenting classical concepts in a way that can be assimilated easily.

The philosophical system/s (darśana) and spiritual practice/s (sādhana) that originated and developed in India (Bhārata) give a way to think (cintana), study and practice (abhyāsa) towards liberation from all sorrow and to explore the nature of human Consciousness (mānava cetana), life itself. Within India, many traditions and practices developed and spread all over, continuing for millennia. All, in their own way, continuously emphasize orienting one's awareness towards seeing the wholeness of one's Self, wholeness of life, the ocean of bliss, the ever-shimmering Consciousness that is the nature of one's Consciousness.

Sāṅkhya Darśana, oldest among the 6 Vedic existential philosophies (aṣṭika darśana),[1] prepares the ground on which Yogic practices takes place. Sāṅkhya creates a basis for Yogic practice (yoga abhyāsa). In the process of Yoga, one goes through Saṃyama[2] gradually, which is required to experience and transcend the understanding of phenomena (tattva krama) and become

---

[1] (1) Nyāya; logic, (2) Vaiśeshika; atomism, (3) Sāṅkhya; enumeration, (4) Yoga; meditation, (5) Mīmāṃsā; critical interpretation, (6) Vedānta; Upaniṣads

[2] The combined simultaneous practice of yogic concentration (dhāraṇā), meditation (dhyāna), and absorption (samādhi)

established in the Self. In the stages of engrossment (sampatti) and realization (samādhi) that is extensively developed in Patañjali's Yoga system, the meditator requires clarity of phenomena (tattvas) and their understanding (lakṣaṇā). Knowing the characteristic or nature of these elements prepares one to Meditate. One sits with clarity and gradually meditates as per the instruction of the Guru on these principles (tattvas). We find this foundation elaborated in the *Sāṅkhyakārikā* and its commentaries. Therefore, it is important to have clarity of foundation and then the process ahead becomes more easeful.

In this book, Suraj-ji brings the traditional approach of understanding the Sāṅkhya Darśana in the classical way, which makes the text easy to understand, and at the same time easy to assimilate the core concepts. For beginners who want to enter into Yogic practice, beginning with a good philosophical basis definitely helps to assimilate Yogic practices. Having a background of traditional studies, and being well versed in the system, Suraj-ji brings out the essence in a way so that everyone can assimilate the concept, and at the same time gain entry in the system. In the present time when orientation towards traditional ways of learning the system is lacking, Suraj-ji is bringing it back through his approach of presentation in this book.

This will definitely help readers to gain entry and connect to the root of Yoga. The essence of Sāṅkhya based on *Sāṅkhyakārikā* and its commentaries, Suraj-ji presents the work in a way so that one can easily gain entry into the system. The text presents the Kārikā in Sanskrit, followed by its transliteration. This shows the authenticity of the text, where one not only sees one view but also has space to see the original text, showing the path of vast tradition. After completion of each topic, presenting the points for reflection will help to get the essence to contemplate, and will help in meditation. The very important aspect is to have orientation towards Self, and that is only through grace. The text plays an important role in it. It helps one to begin questioning. Once one gets clarity of thinking, one can then easily explore the vast tradition horizontally and vertically.

Navkant Juyal

# EDITOR'S NOTE

Although many Yoga teachers may be familiar with the term 'Sāṅkhya' and know it as the philosophical basis for Patañjali's Yoga Sūtras, *Sāṅkhyakārikā* is a text that is barely known in today's modern Yoga world. As a Yoga teacher myself for over 20 years, I have studied Sāṅkhya philosophy and Patañjali's Yoga Sutras extensively and share what I know of the philosophy with budding new Yoga teachers in their training courses.[3] However, this is the first time the full text of *Sāṅkhyakārikā* has come across my path. I feel lucky that my first exposure to it is this lovely translation and commentary by Suraj, written and explained in the simplest way possible, although the subject matter is seemingly deeply complex.

The process of initially reading this text was a journey for me. There were times when my mind felt lost in the complex explanation of Nature. I found myself trying hard to compartmentalize and "figure out" how all the pieces of the puzzle fit together. It left my mind spinning and feeling dense, heavy, and very tamāsic. As the text progressed, the tamāsic feel transformed (via rājas) to sāttva, like an untangling and unfolding of a path that leads straight to the luminous essence of Spirit itself. I could feel the very journey the text explains unfolding in myself as I read it. In this invisible and very sacred way, there is a deep transmission of wisdom held within Suraj's words.

Life (Nature) is a dance of expansion and return, from gross to subtle and subtle to gross, sāttva to tamās and tamās to sāttva. All things exist in order for Consciousness or Spirit to know itself in every way and form possible, and every single form, both manifest and unmanifest, carries the message of the path to Spirit. In other words, we, and everything we experience are in service of Spirit. To take it even one step further, we ARE Spirit experiencing itself in all these different ways and forms.

---

[3] https://www.ekhartyoga.com/articles/browse_all?page=1&contributors=tracey%20uber%20cook

While immersed in the initial stages of learning the 25 principles, my advice is to remember that this is an important step to understanding what the 'not-Self' is. Like in many of the Indic philosophies, this one teaches what 'isn't' before it teaches what 'is', with the eventual realization that everything leads to the exact same thing: Spirit.

As you travel through your journey of reading, understanding, and experiencing the truth of this text, see if you can also feel the unravelling from dense to subtle, from gross to ethereal within the text. There is a certain spaciousness and peace that can be felt in the process. See if you notice this also in yourself, and then see if you can notice this in the world around you: the eternal calling of Spirit for us to return to the knowing of the simple and precious ground of our being.

Tracey Cook

# PUBLISHER'S NOTE

Sāṅkhya is the philosophy originally taught by Kapila, a great Vedic sage whom Swami Vivekananda once called *"the first philosopher of the human race"*. The word Sāṅkhya is related to logic and mathematics and originally had to do with enumeration. It is a systematic philosophical approach to realizing our true nature and overcoming suffering through cultivating a deep understanding of, and differentiation between, Nature and Spirit.

**samyak** = correct understanding that the Self is pure Spirit
**khyāyate** = fully and clearly revealed
samyak + khyāyate = **Sāṅkhya**

All our experiencing is basically subject-object. The subject 'I' am experiencing the collective object as 'all-this' world or universe in general or anything else in particular. Sāṅkhya teaches us that this is correct – that this is how we experience anything and everything. Sāṅkhya clarifies that the subject is Consciousness (Puruṣa/Spirit) and that any object of awareness is matter (Prakṛti/Nature). In the Sāṅkhya model, Spirit is Consciousness and Nature is matter. Spirit is ever the experiencer and Nature is whatever is experienced or experienceable, including our own body and mind. Sāṅkhya declares that you (witness-Consciousness) are the subject or Spirit, and that absolutely everything else is object or Nature.

The important point that Sāṅkhya addresses is that we seem to be confused about the difference between *subject* (Self) and *object* (other). We tend to think, *"I am this body-mind organism. I am these feelings and emotions, thoughts and opinions; I am a product of my psychological conditioning, etc."* Sāṅkhya is here to remind that 'I', the subject, am not any object of Awareness, physical or energetic. The question is, why? Why does this ancient practical philosophy focus on the obvious?

Firstly, what Sāṅkhya teaches, its revelation is logical and based on reason and direct experience, but it is far from obvious. It is a cause of great confusion, out of which all of our ignorance, error, and suffering arise. Secondly, if we can stop ignoring the questions of identity and suffering, then we also will remove the error and the causes of suffering thereby. Confusion and dissatisfaction are experienced by everyone and their presence in the world causes us to try to alleviate or end suffering through logical or discriminative inquiry. In this sense, Nature becomes our teacher, one that demonstrates the truth of Consciousness by redirecting our misguided sense of identity back to pure Spirit.

Yoga in the context of systematic discipline and practice, as detailed by Patañjali in his *Yoga Sutras*, is intimately linked with Sāṅkhya. Sāṅkhya is the underlying spiritual philosophy (knowledge) and Yoga provides the practice (experience) that leads to realizing that the true-Self is not the body-mind or any other object of, or in, Nature, but rather is pure Spirit. Transcendent *knowledge* and experiential *revelation* both have powerful roles to play. Today Yoga is experiencing a worldwide explosion in popularity. Sadly, it seems that the wider and faster Yoga expands, the more disconnected it becomes from its spiritual roots.

**Sāṅkhya** = Discernment + Detachment

**Yoga** as 'Mind-Control' / 'Practice' = Discipline

**Sāṅkhya** + **Yoga** → Desire (for Union)

**Sāṅkhya** + **Yoga** + **Desire** (for Union) = **Yogyatā** (deserving/capable of Union)

Relatively speaking, very few Yoga practitioners even know of the *Yoga Sutras*. Even fewer students and teachers alike have studied the *Yoga Sutras* in-depth or mastered the practices therein. Just as important to a comprehensive study of Yoga, and just as unfortunate, fewer still teach the spiritual component of Sāṅkhya as an integral aspect of Yoga instruction in modern times.

Suraj, with his background in Vedic Logic, Sanskrit, Sāṅkhya, and Advaita Vedānta, provides a systematic approach to studying and understanding Sāṅkhya in this book. Yoga students, teachers, and teacher training courses worldwide will benefit by including the study of Sāṅkhya into their practice. This book is a step in that direction.

J. Erik LaPort

# AUTHOR'S PREFACE

Sāṅkhya is the most ancient form of philosophy. The father of this philosophy school was a great sage from remote antiquity named Kapila. Kapila's father was sage Kardama and his mother was Devahūti. A philosophical discussion between Kapila and his mother Devahūti is found in many Indian mythological texts such as the *Bhāgavata Purāṇa*. We have the mention of Sāṅkhya in many other ancient texts such as the *Mahābhārata* and *Bhagavad-gītā*.

It is understood in Indian tradition that this book (*Mahābhārata*) is five thousand years old (c. 3100 BCE). After winning the Mahābhārata war (the Great War to unify India during remote antiquity), king Yudhiṣṭhira started a new calendar called yugabda. It is 5124 yugabda at the time of writing this book (2023), making Sāṅkhya philosophy at present over 5,000 years old.

Many philosophical texts such as the *Bhagavad-gītā* borrow their philosophical foundation from Sāṅkhya philosophy. The original text written by sage Kapila was called the Sāṅkhya Sutras. Unfortunately, that text no longer exists in its original form.

Later in time, a scholar named Iśvarakṛṣṇa composed a small text named the *Sāṅkhyakārikā*, which is presented here. Currently, the *Sāṅkhyakārikā* is the main source of Sāṅkhya philosophy. The original composition date of this text is unknown, but it is believed that this text is 2-3 thousand years old. This text was translated to Chinese and made available in 569 CE.

The *Sāṅkhyakārikā* is written in the poetry meter called Āryā. It is a beautiful meter, and the poetry is also very exquisite. Those who are fluent in Sanskrit can appreciate the beauty of the original Sanskrit text. The text is composed of 72 passages, (also called 'verses') but the original philosophical views are explained in 70 passages only.

The *Sāṅkhyakārikā* is known for its simplicity. This text gives the reader or student all the necessary information to understand the reality of Self and not-Self to overcome the saṃsāra cycle of suffering without lengthy and complicated philosophical views. It is a small and simple philosophical text that is easy to master in short time. It used to be the primary text for the ancient Yoga schools. Sāṅkhya is well praised as the master of all philosophical schools. It is a *"must study"* text for students of Yoga and Vedānta.

There are two Sanskrit commentaries available on the *Sāṅkhyakārikā* by two great scholars, the 6th century CE philosopher Gauḍapāda, and the 9th/10th century philosopher Vāchaspati Miśra. Gauḍapāda was a master of another philosophical school called Advaita Vedānta. His passages (*Gauḍapāda Kārikā*) on the *Māṇḍūkya Upaniṣad* are very famous and still studied by many people. Gauḍapāda Kārikā is believed to be one of the best books on nondual spiritual philosophy. He is also known as the grandmaster of great Śaṅkārācarya, the systematizer of Advaita Vedānta as it exists today.

Gauḍapāda's commentary on the *Sāṅkhyakārikā* is brief and profound. It was the first and remains the most famous commentary ever written on the *Sāṅkhyakārikā.* In it, he addresses all the principles and philosophical models from the text in a very simple and uncomplicated way.

Vāchaspati Miśra was another great scholar of nondual philosophy. He is well known for his work on the 12 different philosophical schools (of India). He wrote his commentaries on all the 12 philosophical views (materialism, Jainism, four different Buddhist schools, Karma theory, Nyāya school of logic, Vaiśeṣika philosophy, Yoga philosophy, Sāṅkhya philosophy, and Vedānta philosophy). His commentary on the *Sāṅkhyakārikā* is deep and elaborated. He addresses many logical issues, objections, and grammatical points with details. Vāchaspati Miśra's commentary is very much loved by scholars.

It wasn't an easy job to translate the *Sāṅkhyakārikā* into English. One of the challenges was to find English words that can convey the same ideas as the original Sanskrit. There are no English words for some of the Sanskrit words used in the original text. I had to find other ways to express these ideas. I used the Vaman Shivram Apte's *Sanskrit–English Dictionary* when necessary. I find it the best dictionary for Sanskrit available and for this reason, have been using it for past 10 years.

The *Sāṅkhyakārikā* is a very old text and many of its conceptual models are outdated. Science has since provided new models that are widely accepted today. It was challenging to express the original ideas in modern terms, but we can still see the beauty of ancient thinkers though them. The original ancient models were cutting-edge for their time.

Sāṅkhya and Vedānta are the most popular philosophical schools from very ancient times that still exist today. They share many similar ideas with each other, yet they differ on several points of doctrine. Advaita Vedānta is considered as nondual spiritual philosophy, whereas Sāṅkhya falls into the category of dualistic school.

Puruṣa (pure-Consciousness) and Prakṛti (material Nature) are both considered real phenomena in Sāṅkhya philosophy, whereas in Advaita Vedānta, Brahman (pure-Consciousness) alone is real phenomena and Māyā (material Nature) is unreal phenomena, an ever-changing appearance. Both schools accept that Nature is a dynamic equilibrium of three qualities (sāttva, rājas, and tamās) and Spirit (pure-Consciousness) is free of all qualities and without any cause and effect. Both philosophical schools accept that Spirit is actually ever free and unaffected by Nature and its products, yet by association, the qualities of Nature are superimposed on the Spirit. Spirit is ever free from the saṃsāra cycle of suffering. This cycle of suffering is superimposed on Spirit by ignorance; therefore, the superimposition by the mind can be remedied by proper knowledge. Both schools accept that discriminative knowledge of Self and not-Self is sufficient to overcome all the suffering that is caused by misapprehension.

Multiplicity of spirits is accepted by Sāṅkhya to explain the multiplicity of living beings. Conversely, Advaita Vedānta presents the notion of one Spirit, but also multiplicity in the form of 'borrowed' or 'reflected' Consciousness to address the multiplicity of beings. Sāṅkhya prefers to keep its approach simple, practical, and minimalistic. From the Sāṅkhya perspective, it does not matter if one spirit or many exist, or whether or not Nature is real phenomena. Sāṅkhya teaches that it is like someone who is imprisoned does not care whether or not many other prisoners are there too, or if he or she is the only prisoner there. That individual is only interested in his or her own freedom.

Sāṅkhya teaches that Spirit is already free, that the appearance of bondage and suffering is superimposed on it, and that by discriminative understanding of Self and not-Self, one can overcome all the suffering caused by ignorance and error. For Sāṅkhya, the true-Self (Puruṣa) is pure-Spirit in the form of individual witness-Consciousness.

Advaita Vedānta on the other hand, follows a more complex structure. First, Vedānta presents the notion of one Spirit. Only later, to address the issue of multiplicity of being, another notion of *"borrowed"* or *"reflected"* individualized consciousness is introduced. Different Vedānta schools present this notion of borrowed or reflected consciousness in different ways. There are four Vedānta schools that differ from each other on this point, which makes Vedānta somewhat more complicated and difficult to understand. For Advaita Vedānta, the true-Self (Puruṣa) is impersonal universal Consciousness – *supreme Universal-Intelligence* – as the Self of all.

Although the Yoga school is based on Sāṅkhya philosophy, this book is not an instruction manual on Yoga. This book shares philosophical views and a method of analysis that is backed by three means of knowledge – direct perception, reasoning, and testimony. The Yoga school has no philosophy of its own; Yoga borrows the philosophical views of Sāṅkhya and offers additional physical and mental practices to purify and prepare the student for the study and deeper understanding of Sāṅkhya philosophy.

# ACKNOWLEDGMENTS

I offer sincere gratitude to my Sanskrit teacher who taught me this ancient language, which opened the door to the highest spiritual knowledge. In addition, I would also like to thank the other teachers and Swamis who generously shared their knowledge of logic (Nyāya) and spiritual philosophy (Sāṅkhya and Advaita Vedānta). Without this knowledge, this book would not be before you today.

In addition, I would like to thank my friends and classmates Ron and Surya for their friendship and support over the years. To J. Erik LaPort, thank you for encouraging me to write this book, and for including me in your research on Soma of the Ṛgveda and Yajurveda. I must also express gratitude to Vineet, a dear friend and patron, and to my patrons Sananda and Shekinah for their financial support while working on this project.

I am very grateful to Daan and Dorus de Vries for reading this manuscript and for their valuable suggestions. Dorus' sharp eye and corrections helped improve the text greatly.

Lastly, and most importantly, thank you, the reader, for helping to preserve the spiritual origins and basis of Yoga. Now more than ever, as Yoga becomes increasingly popular worldwide, it is important that Yoga preserves and maintains its spiritual heritage as a path to the highest knowledge – the type of knowledge that Liberates.

# Introduction

*"... having thoroughly thought over (this distinctness of the Self),*

*the Self is realized, which is the basis and the illuminator*

*of all the objects (of Awareness) including ego."*

— Kapila to his mother Devahūti

Kapila, a 12 year-old boy, wanted to take the life of a spiritual renunciate and wander the earth by foot. His mother, Devahūti, couldn't understand why anyone would leave a life of pleasure and comfort and become a wandering renunciate. However, she also knew that Kapila was no ordinary person. He was the son of the great sage Kardama, who also lived the life of a renunciate. Therefore, she had to understand why they decided to choose that path.

There must be something greater, more significant, and meaningful, which ordinary people addicted to worldly comforts and pleasures are unable to see. Those who understand extraordinary phenomena and renounce worldly pleasures and comforts without hesitation, what is that extraordinary phenomena that is missing? So mother Devahūti asked Kapila to teach her about that supreme phenomena, so that she too could overcome the suffering and frustration of the mortal world.

What is the true purpose of life? What is world made up of? What is the reality of it? What is the reality of human existence? What is the ultimate Truth? These are a few fundamental questions of human existence. Every human being, both ancient and modern, has these questions in their hearts. Many people live their entire lives without trying to find answers to these questions, and suffer the agony of ignorance without realizing who or what they really are.

The fulfillment of human existence cannot be achieved without answering these questions. We may learn many things about the world, gathering various skills, but if we fail to understand our true nature, it is the biggest loss there is. One who owns everything, but loses the Self, loses everything. One, who realizes the Self by losing everything, actually loses nothing. This is a book about Self-inquiry and Self-realization. Anyone who wants to know himself/herself, and overcome the grief of ignorance, would do well to study what this book teaches.

As a student of philosophy, I always found the Sāṅkhya philosophy very interesting for its simplicity and straightforwardness. Sāṅkhya is the foundation of the Yoga school. All the great masters of Yoga were also Sāṅkhya philosophers. The school of Yoga was invented to facilitate the study of Sāṅkhya. Unfortunately, those who claim to be Yoga students and teachers nowadays know almost nothing about Sāṅkhya as the origin of the Yoga school. Without the vision of Sāṅkhya, Yoga is like a blind bird flying without direction.

Therefore, I was encouraged to write a brief commentary on Sāṅkhya as the spiritual foundation of Yoga by my friend and colleague, J. Erik LaPort. It wasn't an easy task to translate and comment on this book. I needed to face several challenges as I worked on this project. I studied two different Sanskrit commentaries on *Sāṅkhyakārikā* by Gauḍapāda and Vāchaspati Miśra. I also studied the teaching of a great scholar from Kailash Ashram, in Rishikesh. It was challenging to express some of the ancient concepts in modern English language, but I had help from my mentor to do so.

Sāṅkhya is a very ancient school of philosophy that even now withstands the scrutiny of time, and helps the generation of humanity to find the answers to fundamental questions of human existence, to overcome the struggle and suffering of life. It is one of the most beautiful and simplest forms of philosophy. I find myself very fortunate for having the opportunity and skillset to present this ancient book to the modern world. The *Sāṅkhyakārikā* has helped many sincere seekers and students of Yoga throughout history. I hope that this new English translation will perform its service as well today as the original Sanskrit text did in the past. Unfortunately, Yoga schools nowadays rarely teach Sāṅkhya philosophy, which is the very basis of Yoga. I sincerely hope this new edition will help to restore the original order of Yoga backed by the profound wisdom of Sāṅkhya.

# INTRODUCTION

This book begins with inquiry to address the different kinds of suffering of human existence. In order to overcome the suffering, the root-cause is analyzed by logical reasoning, and the means of its removal is also explained. Sāṅkhya divides its approach to address a philosophical view using ten principles. The book first establishes primordial Nature as the cause of everything. The primordial cause consists of three qualities, and it is ever changing. Next, we establish the oneness or interconnectedness of Nature, meaning there is only one primordial cause for a variety of effects. Then we will see the usefulness of Nature as cause and effect is explained. We'll then go deeper into an analysis of Self and not-Self, differentiating Spirit (Self) and Nature (not-Self). Next, we will learn the conceptual model to understand Nature with all its effects to the extent where it is understood clearly and vividly, including its functions and usefulness. The remainder of the text takes the reader to ever more subtle levels of understanding Spirit, Divine Union, Reality, Realization, and Freedom. Admittedly, the text can be a bit confusing in the beginning, but if the reader continues until the end of the text, the whole of Sāṅkhya philosophy has a way of coming together and making sense in an intuitive way.

To study Sāṅkhya is to learn a higher knowledge, the type of knowledge that liberates. Naturally, the question may arise, "How does knowledge Liberate?" To become free from suffering, we must need to know the root-cause of suffering. Only after identifying and understanding that root-cause, can we look forward to overcoming the suffering. What is the single root-cause of the entirety of human suffering? The answer, ignorance! How do you overcome ignorance? By knowledge only!

There is no other way to overcome ignorance other than knowledge. Any other means of attempting to overcome suffering without knowledge is a foolish undertaking. It is said in spiritual philosophy that if one could roll up space like a Yoga-mat, they would be able to overcome suffering without Self-knowledge. However, such a feat being impossible, we turn to knowledge. If we are lost in a deep dark cave, suffering because of it, there is no other way of overcoming the suffering other than lighting a light. Knowledge is like lighting an inner light that overcomes the darkness.

Quite naturally, there can be objections to Sāṅkhya philosophy's approach to spirituality. Firstly, *why should we not rely on science and psychology in the pursuit of Truth?* The cycle of cause and effect, of pleasure and pain, reward and punishment, is understood as the saṃsāra cycle of suffering. It is bondage, and staying in this cycle is real suffering. All worldly skills exist to reinforce and facilitate the continuation of the cycle, including science and psychology. Trying to overcome the cycle using these modern tools is like trying to put out fire using gasoline. Science and psychology only strengthens the subject-object division. Any benefit that science and psychology may offer will always be only temporary and ever-changing over time. Sāṅkhya philosophy on the other hand, helps to overcome subject-object division, which is always based on Self-ignorance. Sāṅkhya reveals the phenomena free from cause-effect relationship.

Secondly, *Sāṅkhya philosophy teaches that knowledge alone liberates. How does knowledge liberate?* According to Sāṅkhya, suffering exists because of body-mind identification. Body, mind, senses are parts of nature, thus they are always continuously changing. They are (1) inert without Spirit to enliven them, and (2) they are objects of perception. Spirit, on the other hand, is free of the cause-effect relationship, relative, and changeless. Spirit is sensitive or conscious phenomenon. Taking such a temporary and ever-changing body-mind organism as the identity of the Self is delusion. The root cause of error that leads to the delusion of false identification is Self-ignorance. Therefore, ultimately self-ignorance is the cause of all suffering. Only knowledge can remove the ignorance, like only light can remove darkness, and not anything else. Self-ignorance as the cause of all suffering can only be remedied by Self-knowledge. Sāṅkhya presents the knowledge of Spirit as the true identity of Self and Nature as not-Self to realize freedom from all human suffering.

Finally, *what good is a philosophy that has no concept of God in it?* Sāṅkhya philosophy is presented to overcome suffering and frustration based on ignorance. God is understood as the controller and punisher in most religions today. The concept of God was introduced as the creator of the world or creation. According to Sāṅkhya, Nature is the material cause of everything. Spirit is unreactive; therefore, it cannot be the Controller or Creator of anything. Spirit in the Sāṅkhya view is not synonymous with God as generally understood. A root-cause of suffering is fear. Fear is the basis of all other causes of human suffering. God is typically associated with fear, and specifically a fear of God. We are not attacking God, but rather the human concept of God. Fear is the cause of bondage, wherever there is bondage there cannot be freedom and suffering remains thereby. Therefore, Sāṅkhya provides a philosophy free from the concept of God in the role of Creator or Controller. According to Sāṅkhya, there are only two principles – Self and not-Self. Self is Spirit, which is unreactive and changeless. Not-Self is Nature, which is reactive and ever-changing, therefore neither of these principles can be called 'God'. Sāṅkhya addresses God in the conventional sense as an unnecessary concept that causes more problems than the concept solves.

This book, *THE SPIRITUAL FOUNDATION OF YOGA: Understanding Nature and Spirit* is an open invitation for Yoga practitioners, teachers, enthusiasts, and everyone interested in spiritual philosophy to expand their understanding in this field by studying it. It will improve not only your practice but also your overall life experience and expression. It is my genuine wish that you, dear reader, realize what Sāṅkhya promises: higher wisdom, the end of life's suffering, Self-realization, and spiritual freedom. Blessings, and may this book be of service to you on your journey.

# 1

# The Purpose of Inquiry

दुःखत्रयाभिघाताज्जिज्ञासा तदभिघातके हेतौ ।
दृष्टे सापार्था चेन्नैकान्तात्यन्ततोऽभावात् ॥ १ ॥

duḥkha-trayā-abhighātāt-jijñāsā tat-abhighātake hetau ।
dṛṣṭe sā-apārthā cet na-ekāntā-atyantataḥ abhāvāt ॥

– 1 –

*Because of association with three types of suffering,*
*there is inquiry (presented here) into the means of their removal.*
*(Objection): If other means are available, then this inquiry is useless.*
*(Response): No. They [such means] are neither certain, nor permanent.*

### *3-Types of Suffering*

**Q**: When you say *"three types of suffering"*, how do you categorize them?

**A**: it is not possible to talk about each and every problem, pain, and suffering individually. We categorize them so we can address them more effectively. All types of pain and suffering fall into three main categories:

1. ***Personal (inner) suffering*** further divided into two sub-categories, as:
    a. *physical suffering* such as illness, injury, disease, etc.
    b. *mental suffering* such as fear, worry, stress, anxiety, mental illness, etc.
2. ***Circumstantial (outer) suffering*** caused by other living beings, like criminals, animals, etc.
3. ***Natural (extraordinary) suffering*** caused by disasters, things outside of our control, etc.

Therefore, one should desire into the means of their removal.

## *Inquiry and the Pursuit of Happiness*

**Q**: Why study philosophy, what is the origin of all philosophies; what does this philosophy have to offer?

**A**: First, we must understand the very meaning of the word *'philosophy'*. Philosophy generally means *'knowledge'*[4] or *'love for knowledge'*. The Sanskrit word for philosophy is *'darśanam'*, which means *'seeing'* or *'means of knowledge'*. Now that we understand what is meant by the word philosophy, we can begin to answer some important questions.

What is the true meaning of human existence? What is the purpose of life? How can we find the fulfillment in this life expression? These are some fundamental questions that have existed throughout human history, and will continue to exist so long as humanity does. These are the questions every human being has in their heart – no matter how primitive or sophisticated – and which everybody is trying to answer in their own way. To question philosophically in this way is what is meant by the word *'inquiry'* – Self-inquiry, Truth-inquiry, Spiritual-inquiry, etc.

Philosophy is a means of answering these questions so one can find satisfaction and fulfillment in one's heart. In fact, any attempt to answer these questions can be considered as philosophical inquiry. We study philosophy so we can find the answers to these fundamental questions of human existence.

We can see that people are not happy with their lives in general. Everybody is searching for something. We have all kinds of ideas and concepts about life, and search for happiness in so many different directions. We pursue money, sex, success, fame, relationship, social status, etc. thinking these might help to overcome that unhappiness, but in reality, it doesn't work. The more we get, the more we want, and the more we want, the more unhappy we feel.

Think carefully and you will find that every human being is interested in only one thing, in the complete removal of all suffering. Ask many people what they really want and the most common answer is always *"I just want to be happy"*.

---

[4] i.e., 'wisdom', higher or the highest knowledge

Which is to say, we all want to be free from afflictions, frustrations and misery. In fact, the very fulfillment of human existence is in overcoming suffering and discovering the true and uninterrupted happiness, joy, and peace, that comes from within.

How can we overcome suffering, pain and frustration, is it even possible? To overcome any problem we need to understand the root cause of that problem. By resolving the root cause, we can easily overcome the problem. If the suffering is from an illness, rather than treating symptoms, we can find the root cause of the illness and address that. This is the proper and most effective way to overcome the suffering caused by the illness.

Now the fundamental question is, is it possible to overcome all suffering, pain, and frustration? The answer is yes. Great sages like Kapila and Patañjali have found a way to overcome all the collective suffering altogether. They have found the root cause of all human suffering and they also presented the means for removal of its root cause. They have tested this method of inquiry in their own lives. They overcame all suffering and pain, and discovered independent uninterrupted happiness and peace in their own hearts. Their discovery is what is presented here, this being the same method of inquiry so others can also benefit from it.

Without realizing the root cause of all the suffering, it is not possible to overcome the suffering just as disease cannot be treated without knowing the cause of it. If we can comprehend the root cause of all the suffering, then we can confidently put effort towards the removal of that cause using the appropriate measures. Moreover, by the removal of all suffering, we can realize that independent uninterrupted happiness and joy within. Therefore, we can learn and apply this inquiry to discover the appropriate means to overcome all suffering.

### *Objection: Why Not Use Conventional Means?*

The worldly objection is this: If there are other means available (the ordinary or conventional means commonly tried) to overcome suffering, why should we bother with complex philosophical methods of inquiry?

Personal suffering is addressed with proper medical treatment. When we suffer from physical pain, we consult a doctor, take medications, adjust diet, etc. When there is a mental disorder, we can seek help from a psychologist or psychiatrist. Circumstantial problems can be dealt with proper measures. With predatorial fears, we can carry a weapon, or secure a protected place to live away from dangerous animals or people, etc. Natural and supernatural problems can be dealt with by the use of technology to our advantage avoid or minimize the effects of disasters and calamities or to survive extreme atmospheric conditions, etc. These are some of the conventional means of alleviating suffering. Philosophical inquiry reveals these methods to be useless. Why is this so?

### *Response: Conventional Means are Just Temporary Fixes*

The philosophical response is this: No, the conventional way is not right because those ordinary means are neither certain (there's no guarantee that they will work) nor permanent (if they do work, the fix is only ever temporary).

We can see that not all forms of disease or mental illness can be treated. If somehow we can manage to overcome some of the physical and mental problems, there is no guarantee that the problem/s will not recur. Sometimes it can even take years of treatment to overcome even a simple illness, some of which are even incurable, or cost of treatment is so expensive that not everyone can afford it.

It is not possible for everyone to carry a weapon everywhere for protection. It takes years of practice to develop and master skills of self-defense. There is no guarantee of being able to protect against external threats from overpowering forces beyond our control. Not all supernatural problems can be solved by technology either. Some natural disasters are so powerful that we cannot prevent them, or afford the technology required to do so. Sometimes even technology can be a cause of threat, suffering, and problems. We use technology to create and fight wars, to kill, to commit mass destruction, etc. so technology is not always the answer to help overcome suffering.

This method of philosophical inquiry on the other hand, is the best solution there is. It not only helps to overcome all forms of collective suffering all at once, but it permanently removes suffering to the degree that it never arises again. Therefore, those who are interested in overcoming suffering once and for all will benefit from this method of inquiry.

दृष्टवदानुश्रविकः स ह्यविशुद्धिक्षयाऽतिशययुक्तः ।
तद्विपरीतः श्रेयान् व्यक्ताऽव्यक्तज्ञविज्ञानात् ॥ २॥

dṛṣṭavat-ānuśravikaḥ saḥ hi-aviśuddhi-kṣayā-atiśaya-yuktaḥ ।
tat-viparītaḥ śreyān vyaktāḥ avyakta-jña-vijñānāt ॥

– 2 –

*As the seen (conventional means inadequate for removing suffering)*
*so are the unseen (extraordinary or religious means)*
*because they are defective, impermanent, and full of comparison.*
*On the other hand, this understanding*
*of the manifest, unmanifest and the seer is superior.*

***Objection: What about Religion to End Suffering?***

We can well understand that the available worldly or conventional means are inadequate for the removal of suffering, but we've all heard of some extraordinary or religious means that can help a person to overcome suffering by attaining heaven. Perhaps this world is full of pain, suffering, and affliction, but heaven is different from this world. It is full of pleasures and happiness (or so we are told). This world is mortal but heaven is described as eternal, therefore if we want to be free from all kinds of suffering, we should follow a religious path in an attempt to attain or guarantee a permanent place in heaven, free from suffering and misery. This extraordinary means is available to overcome suffering, and therefore there is no need to go through this inquiry.

***Response: Conventional Means are Just Temporary Fixes***

There are many shortcomings and defects in the very pursuit of heaven. First, the very existence of heaven is questionable. We cannot say with any degree of certainty whether such a place really exists or not. Even if we could be certain that heaven really does exist, and furthermore that it is also possible to attain such a heaven through religious practices, it is of no use to anyone right now because it can only be attained after death. No living being (we are told) is allowed into heaven. Therefore, suffering and misery that exists here and now still remains and is therefore unresolved.

Second, religious practices are not easy to perform. There are many rules specific to each different religion, which is highly variable from one to another. Even if we could be sure of the correct form, some of the very practices of religious expression can create lot of problems and frustration for others. For example, violence to other living beings is clearly involved in the practice of religious rituals that include animal sacrifice, subjugating others, etc. Much conflict, violence, and bloodshed has transpired in the name of religion.

There is common misconception that heaven is permanent and therefore the happiness and pleasures there will last forever. Heaven is spoken of as long lasting in comparison with this world. Such views place heaven in time (after death) and place (not here). There is a simple universal rule – anything that arises and exists in time and space, eventually comes to an end. Even heaven is no exception to this rule.

Somehow, we might manage to follow all the heavenly rules and not perform any mischief to secure our place in heaven, we will still be unhappy there, because of comparison. There will be other people in heaven as well. Who worshipped more effectively, with more love and devotion? Whose religious notions are more correct? Can we compare the different occupants of heaven, or are there different heavens? Are there different degrees of comfort and pleasure, better rewards for better work? Will there be authority, social classes, and status there too? If comparisons can exist in heaven, will there also be different degrees of happiness there? This pursuit of heaven is also inadequate in the removal of all kinds of suffering. On the other hand, spiritual inquiry to understand the manifest (Nature as effects), the unmanifest (Nature as *Primordial Cause*), and the seer (pure-Consciousness), is superior because it will certainly lead to a comprehensive understanding of suffering – its origins and purpose – and thereby end suffering entirely.

Obviously, we cannot change the world to suit our needs. There will be hot and cold weather, diseases and physical pain, etc. Pain and discomfort are a part of life. Not everyone is going to behave accordingly, and thus actions of one might harm another. However, we can choose not to suffer these afflictions. While it is impossible for a person to change the entire world, it is possible to change our mindset and thereby our response to it. Physical pain caused by aging etc., is unavoidable, but we can choose not to suffer, through a change in mindset, attitude, and approach. There is a story of a prince who wanted to cover the entire earth with leather so he could protect his feet from getting hurt, but he did not realize that this same effect could be achieved by simply wearing a pair of sandals. We cannot remove the cause of pain in the world, but we can change how we approach it ourselves.

There is only a single root cause of all human suffering – Self-ignorance. We suffer because we do not know our true nature. We are badly identified with 'not-Self'. Although it may not seem like it at the beginning of our inquiry, clear discernment between the 'true-Self' and the 'not-Self' is the way to overcome suffering caused by ignorance and false identification. When we begin to awaken to, and fully realize, our true immortal nature, free from qualities of the body-mind and sense complex, we come to realize freedom from afflictions and suffering due to falsely identifying with them. Therefore, Self-realization is the means by which we overcome all suffering. Self-knowledge is impossible without understanding the nature of 'not-Self'. It is important to understand and clearly differentiate both the 'not-Self' and the 'true-Self' through spiritual inquiry and finally realize the Truth of who we are.

मूलप्रकृतिरविकृतिर्महदाद्याः प्रकृतिविकृतयः सप्त ।
षोडशकस्तु विकारो न प्रकृतिर्न विकृतिः पुरुषः॥ ३॥

mūlaprakṛtiḥ avikṛtiḥ mahadādyāḥ prakṛti-vikṛtayaḥ sapta ।
ṣoḍaśakaḥ tu vikāraḥ na prakṛtiḥ na vikṛtiḥ puruṣaḥ ॥

– 3 –

*The Primordial Cause is not created by anything.*
*Intellect, etc. (+ 6 others), 7 are causes as well as effects.*
*The other 16 are only effects (and not a cause).*
*Pure consciousness is neither cause nor effect (of anything).*

A comprehensive model is given as an introduction so that we can easily understand the difference between 'true-Self' and 'not-Self'. Here we must understand that the focus is not on the model, nor the numbers of elements in the given model. The focus is to differentiate between the 'true-Self' and the 'not-Self'. Sāṅkhya's conceptual model of Nature and Spirit has 25 elements in its model, 24 of which comprise the 'not-Self' and only 1 is the 'true-Self'.

Yoga is similar to Sāṅkhya in that it accepts 26 elements (the standard 25 + 1 more, Īśvara/God) in the Yogic model, where also there is only one 'true-Self' and all other elements comprise the 'not-Self'. Therefore, it really does not matter how many elements are given as the conceptual model so long as it helps one to realize the difference between the 'true-Self' and 'not-Self'.

There are only two things to understand clearly – 'true-Self' and 'not-Self. The 'not-Self' is explained first so we can understand the 'true-Self' and differentiate the two. Sāṅkhya's model of the 'not-Self' is made up of 24 components – 1 Nature + 7 transactional principles + 16 effects = 24 principles.

There is a *Primordial Cause* for everything, with itself not being an effect of anything else. It is the original root of all matter, the creative principle in Nature (pradhāna), and the prime mover. It is an equilibrium of three qualities present in all things, beings, and events: (1) *sāttva or 'illumining quality'* = goodness, serenity, harmony, (2) *rājas or 'active quality'* = passion, ambition, action, and (3) *tamās or 'dark and limiting quality'* = ignorance, inertia, laziness.

## 3 QUALITIES (GUṆAS) OF ENERGETIC-EQUILIBRIUM IN NATURE

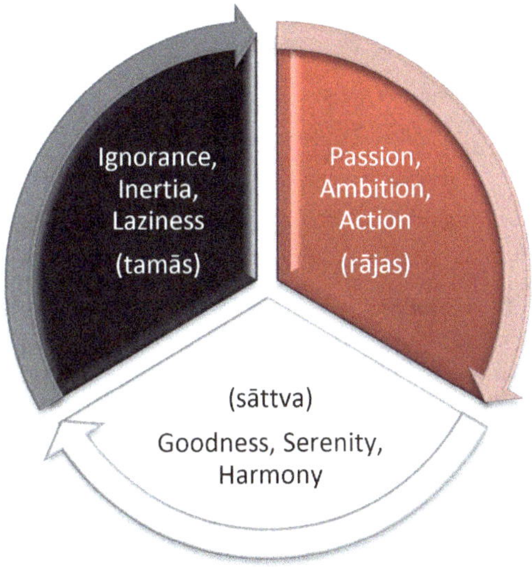


From that *Primordial Cause*, an effect is born. The intellect (thinking faculty), and from that intellect another effect is born, ego (individualized 'I-sense'). Therefore, the intellect is cause (for the ego) as well as an effect (of the *Primordial Cause*). From that ego, five primordial potentials are born. This is why the ego is also both cause and an effect. From those five primordial (subtle) potential elements, five (gross) elements, (space, air, fire, water, and earth) are born, therefore, these 7 elements or aspects of Nature (1 intellect + 1 ego + 5 potentials) are both causes as well as effects, which is to say they are transactional.

## 7 TRANSACTIONAL (CAUSE + EFFECT) ASPECTS OF NATURE

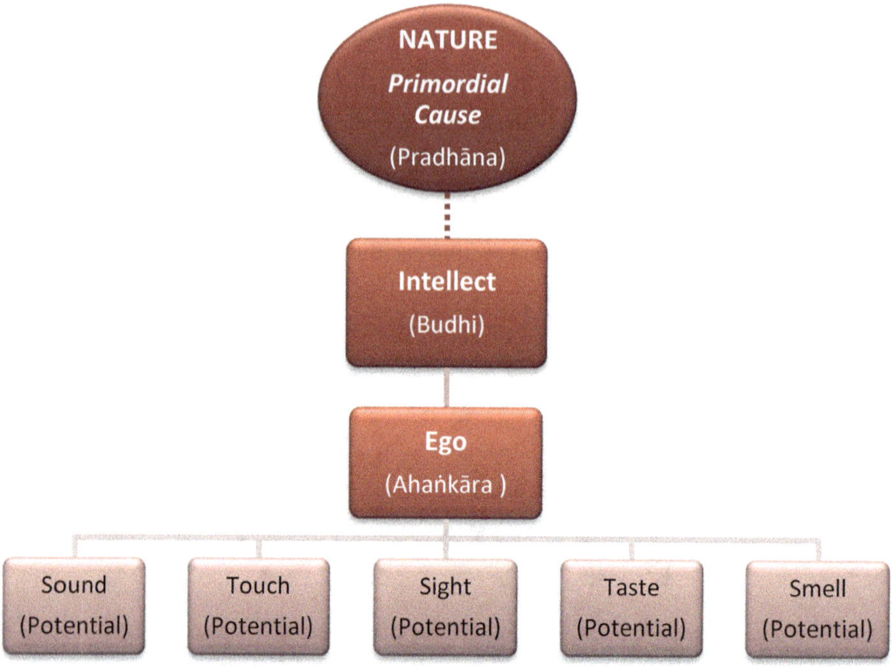


## 16 EFFECTS IN NATURE

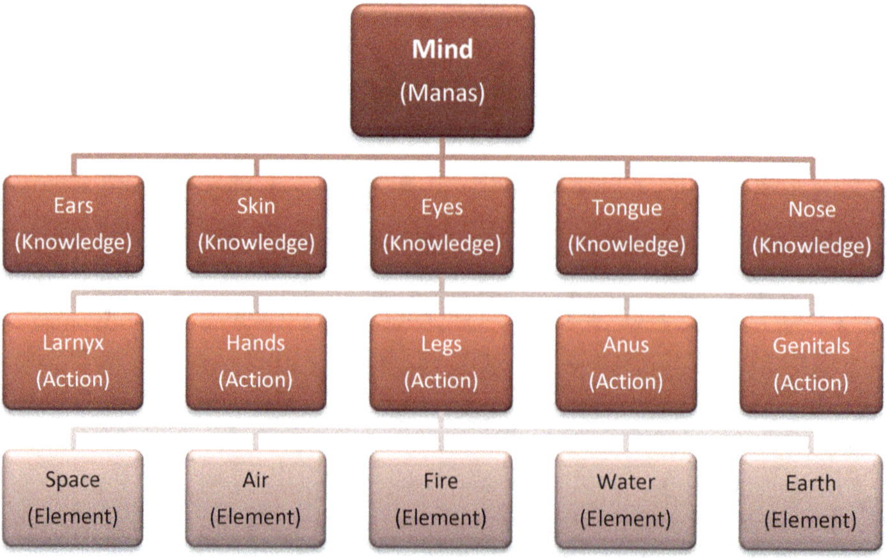

There are 16 other elements or aspects that are effects of the *Primordial Cause* + the other 7 causal aspects, but these 16 are not causes for any other elements (aspects). These include 1 mind, 5 sense organs[5] (eye, ear, nose, tongue, skin), 5 organs of action[6] (hands, legs, larynx, genital, anus), and 5 elements of creation (space, air, fire, water, earth).

All of these 24 elements or aspects constitute human experiencing and fall into the category of the 'not-Self' according to the Sāṅkhya model. Today, science has provided us with so many different models for the body-mind organism and the universe as a whole. Does this make Sāṅkhya's models irrelevant? Absolutely not. Regardless of how, or by what models, we understand Nature, taken as a whole it still is categorized as the 'not-Self'. On the other hand, there is 1 other element, the 25th principle in the model to consider – pure-Consciousness, or pure-Spirit (Puruṣa) – which is neither cause for anything, nor an effect of anything. It alone is the 'true-Self'.

> **Āsurī asks Kapila**, *"What is separate?"*[7]
>
> **Kapila replies**: *"Separate, O Āsurī, is the Puruṣa, the 25th principle, the knower of the field (of awareness) ... pure-Spirit is different from everything ... the field is one thing, the knower of the field is another, (it is) the Puruṣa principle, the 25th principle."*
>
> — *Mahabharata (Southern Edition)*, Dialogue between Āsurī and Kapila

> "Whoever realizes the 25 principles becomes the highest Self, is immortal. Liberated from the flow of Nature, they attain equality with the highest."
>
> — *Mahabharata (Southern Edition)*, Kapila

---

[5] 5 cognitive senses or 5 sense organs, hereafter referred to simply as 'senses' or '5 senses'

[6] 5 active instruments or 5 organs of action, hereafter referred to simply as 'organs' or '5 organs'

[7] Here, the word *'separate'* means independent or non-relative, beyond cause-effect.

## *Points for Reflection*

- The first passage of Chapter 1 gives a compelling case for spiritual life with the promise of overcoming life's suffering in all its forms.[8] Sāṅkhya is given as the solution.
- The primary Sāṅkhya reflective meditation technique (tattvābhyāsa) involves a logical inquiry and clear understanding of the 25 principles. These 25 principles collectively are sub-categories of manifest and unmanifest Nature (Prakṛti), and pure-Consciousness the seer or witness, here called Spirit (Puruṣa).
- The initial meditation is to memorize the 25 principles. The 25 principles address the true-Self (Spirit), the not-Self and the objective world (Nature). Sāṅkhya's meditation program begins by analyzing the not-Self, which is to say an investigation into Sāṅkhya's definition of Nature first, how to accurately identify what is meant by the not-Self.
- Sāṅkhya philosophy is classified into a concise conceptual teaching model, called "The 60 Ideas" (Ṣaṣṭitantra). The 60 ideas include 10 fundamental principles for understanding Nature and Spirit + 50 additional topics concerning spiritual attainments, ignorance, and error. A complete list of "The 60 Ideas", along with chapter references, is enumerated on pages 100 and 101 of this book.

[8] Chapter divisions are by the author. The original text does not contains chapter breaks.

2

# The Way of Logical Inquiry

दृष्टमनुमानमाप्तवचनं च सर्वप्रमाणसिद्धत्वात् ।
त्रिविधं प्रमाणमिष्टं प्रमेयसिद्धिः प्रमाणाद्धि ॥ ४ ॥

dṛṣṭam-anumānam-āptavacanaṃ ca sarva-pramāṇa-siddhatvāt ।
trividhaṃ pramāṇam-iṣṭaṃ prameya-siddhiḥ pramāṇāt-dhi ॥

– 4 –

*Everything is established (known) by means of knowledge.*
*Direct perception, inference, and testimony (from a trustworthy source),*
*these three means of knowledge are accepted,*
*since the establishment of an object is only possible*
*by a valid means of knowledge.*

Everything that we know and want to know can only be known through a 'valid means of knowledge' (pramāṇa). Any information not acquired by valid means will not be accepted as valid knowledge. It will be considered deceptive and false information or, in some cases, fantasy.

We must understand the true-Self, not-Self, and the difference between the two to be free from suffering. Without the proper knowledge and understanding of these, we cannot be free from suffering caused by ignorance and false identification. Therefore, valid knowledge of Nature (Prakṛti) and Spirit (Puruṣa) must come from valid means of knowledge.

The question is, *"How can we realize the Truth of Nature and Spirit?"* What are the means to gain correct understanding? All valid knowledge acquired in worldly transactions is due to these three means of knowledge – direct perception, inference, and verbal testimony from a trustworthy source. In spiritual inquiry, we also apply the same three means of gaining knowledge. When we gain knowledge through direct experience, we call it '*perception*'.

When we gain knowledge indirectly through association with other valid knowledge, we call it *'inference'*. When we gain knowledge from an authoritative source, we call it *'testimony'* by transmission through hearing or listening.

Other thinkers accept some other means of knowledge in addition, but those means are merely sub-categories of these three. There is no need to make things more complicated by longer lists. Sāṅkhya's approach seems to say that it is best to keep the inquiry uncomplicated and straightforward.

The primary aim of our inquiry is to come to a clear and deep discernment or differentiation between Nature and Spirit. Such understanding is only possible by a valid means of knowledge. Without a valid means, we cannot conclude the fundamental nature of these. It is essential to understand what these 'valid means' are, and how they operate. Think of a 'valid means' as a tool or instrument that helps us explore deeper. In our spiritual inquiry, we will use all three.

प्रतिविषयाऽध्यवसायो दृष्टं त्रिविधमनुमानमाख्यातम् ।
तल्लिङ्गिपुर्वकमाप्तश्रुतिराप्तवचनन्तु ॥ ५॥

prati-viṣayādhyavasāyaḥ dṛṣṭaṃ trividham-anumānam-ākhyātam ।
tat-liṅga-liṅgi-pūrvakam-āptaśrutiḥ āptavacanaṃ tu ॥

– 5 –

*The perception of sense objects through respective senses*
*is understood as direct perception.*
*Inference, which is in the form of indicator and indicated*
*is of three types.*
*Verbal testimony from a reliable source*
*is understood as trustworthy words (a means for valid knowledge).*

What are the characteristics of these means of knowledge, and how do they function?

*Direct perception* means the apprehension of sense-objects (sound, touch, form, taste, and smell) through their respective cognitive senses (ear, skin, eyes, tongue, and nose). Senses must come into direct contact with their objects for perception to occur. Without this direct contact between senses and objects, perception is impossible. Therefore, this means of knowledge is called 'direct perception'. Direct perception is the primary means of knowledge; all other means of knowledge, like inference and words, depend on direct perception for their function.

*Logical inference* occurs when an object is unavailable for direct perception, yet we understand it by proper reasoning. This reasoning is threefold – (1) *preceding*, (2) *remaining*, and (3) *similar*.

1. When we can infer that there will be rain today by looking at the clouds based on our previous experience of clouds and rain, this is an example of preceding reasoning.

2. When we can taste a few drops of seawater and conclude that the rest of the seawater is also salty, this is an example of remaining reasoning.

3. When we can see a mango tree with fruit and infer that the other mango trees are also fruiting during the same season, this is an example of similar reasoning.

4. This inference-reasoning contains two elements: (1) an indicator, and (2) indicated. They both can be reasoned by each other.

5. We can reason that a man is a warrior by seeing a sword and shield. The sword and shield serve as an indicator. The indicated (warrior) is reasoned by the indicator (sword and shield). Warriors are associated with swords and shields. Swords and shields are associated with warriors.

6. We can reason by looking at a police officer that he has a badge and a gun. The indicator (badge and gun) is reasoned by the indicated (police officer). Police officers are associated with badges and guns. Badges and guns are associated with police officers.

7. Verbal testimony from a reliable and trustworthy source like Veda (words of great sages with deep wisdom) is a valid means of knowledge. A more typical example might be a traveler who has been out of contact with their family for some time and can come to an understanding about a birth or death of a family member by the words of a trustworthy friend.

सामान्यतस्तु दृष्टादतीन्द्रियाणां प्रतीतिरनुमानात् ।
तस्मादपि चाऽसिद्धं परोक्षमाप्ताऽगमात्सिद्धम् ॥ ६ ॥

sāmānyataḥ tu dṛṣṭāt-atīndriyāṇāṃ pratītiḥ anumānāt ।
tasmādapi cā-siddhaṃ parokṣam-āpta-āgamāt-siddham ॥

– 6 –

*Conviction of things that are beyond the range of direct perception can be reasoned/inferred with general observation. Conviction/understanding that cannot be accomplished by reasoning can be acquired by words of trustworthy source.*

Why do we use multiple means of knowledge, and what is accomplished by which? The scope of direct perception is limited. Not everything can be understood and known by direct perception, which is why other means of knowledge are applied to arrive at things that are not known otherwise.

Things beyond the scope of direct perception can be reasoned and inferred with the help of general observation. We can look at the smoke on a distant mountain and infer the presence of fire based on previous observations that fire and smoke typically go together. This general observation helps us draw conclusions about an object that is unavailable by direct perception.

Nature (Pradhāna) and Spirit (Puruṣa) are unavailable for direct perception. Therefore, we infer them with the help of general observation. We can look at the intellect, ego, and mind, etc., which are of the three qualities (sāttva, rājas, tamās) and infer there to be a *Primordial Cause* for all of these as having three qualities, much the same way one can look at a silk cloth (effect) and infer the material cause of it (silk thread), with the help of general observation of cause and an effect.

Intellect, ego, mind, etc., are collectively an effect of the *Primordial Cause* (Nature). They are inert though they appear sentient. Therefore, we can infer or reason that a different element (Spirit) is present, is conscious, and which animates or enlivens them, causing them to appear sentient thereby. The moon has no light of its own, yet it appears to be luminous, therefore we can infer or reason that there is another source of light by which the moon appears to shine.

Those things that we do not apprehend by reasoning, we can understand by verbal testimony of a trustworthy source. For example, we gain much of our accepted understanding of science through hearing what scientists have discovered even though we have neither directly perceived nor inferred such knowledge ourselves. We trust the authoritative source/s of the knowledge to be valid.

अतिदूरात्सामीप्यादिन्द्रियघातान्मनोनवस्थानात् ।
सौक्ष्म्याद्व्यवधानादभिभवात्समानाभिहाराच्च ॥ ७ ॥

atidūrāt sāmīpyāt-indriyaghātāt-mano-anavasthānāt ।
saukṣmyāt-vyavadhānāt-abhibhavāt samānābhihārāt-ca ॥

**– 7 –**

*(Objects may not be perceived due to circumstances, such as ... )*
*(1) being at great distance, (2) having great proximity/nearness,*
*(3) weakness of sense organs, (4) absence of mind or lack of attention,*
*(5) object being subtle, (6) obstructed or intervened by something,*
*(7) being overpowered by something, or (8) intermixed in equal things.*

### *Objection: If Something Has Never Been Perceived, Does It Exist?*

Spirit and Nature (*Primordial Cause*) are not available to perception, and (imaginary) things that are not seen by anybody do not exist. If they had existed, they would have been perceived. They are not perceived; therefore, Spirit and Nature do not exist.

### *Response: Many Things are Not Perceived, Yet Do Exist*

There are things that do exist, yet remain outside of direct perception due to these 8 limitations. These are limitations of perception as a means of knowledge. Perception's limitation does not invalidate the existence of an object.

1. ***Too Far***: When an object is at great distance, it may not be perceived by direct perception such as the way someone living in different country cannot be seen with the eyes directly. Stars and planets exist at great distances from us, yet are not perceived directly. Our sphere of perception is actually quite small.

2. ***Too Near***: if an object is very close, it may not be perceived. Eyelashes exist very near the eyes, yet we don't see them with our own eyes.

3. ***Sensory Limitations***: if there is a weakness with a sense organ, existing things will not be perceived. For example, the blind cannot see forms or colors, the deaf cannot hear sound, etc.

4. ***Cognitive Limitations***: if attention is otherwise engaged, things will not be perceived. Those with a scattered or distracted mind do not see things that are presented them.

5. ***Too Small or Subtle***: if an object is too small, it will not be perceived much the same way small particles and microorganisms cannot be seen by the naked eye. Alternatively, an object might be too subtle for human perception, such as radio waves, our mobile phone signal, electromagnetic forces, etc.

6. ***Hidden***: purposefully or not, if an object is obstructed or intervened by something it will not be perceived in the same way that things behind the curtain are not seen, hidden from view.
7. ***Overpowered***: If an object is overpowered by something, it will not be seen much the same way stars and moon are not seen during the daytime due to being overpowered by sunlight.
8. ***Intermixed/Camouflaged***: if an object is intermixed with things of equal or similar appearance, it will not be perceived, such as how a single fish hides within a school of the same, birds in a flock, or a familiar voice being drowned out in a large crowd.

If any of these limitations are present, even an existing thing will not be perceived. We cannot simply conclude that things that are not available for direct perception do not exist – claiming, *"If we don't see it, it's not there"*. Just because we cannot see something, doesn't mean it is not there.

The *Primordial Cause* can be likened to wind. Nobody will ever deny the existence of wind – but equally, nobody has ever seen wind. We feel wind on our face. We see its effects in the swaying trees or blowing of debris. We hear it as it howls down the valley or through the branches. We perceive the effects, but do not see the cause. We cannot deny the cause and therefore infer the cause to be wind.

Today with modern technology, this understanding is even more relevant. Nobody has ever seen a mobile phone signal with direct perception, yet we can measure, capture, and use it. Like the wind analogy above, we can directly perceive the effects, but not the cause, the microwave signal remaining hidden to direct perception but still present all around us. We cannot deny the mobile phone's signal and therefore infer the cause to be a telecommunication signal tower somewhere nearby.

सौक्ष्म्यात्तदनुपलब्धिर्नाऽभावात् कार्यतस्तदुपलब्धेः ।
महदादि तच्च कार्यं प्रकृतिविरूपं सरूपं च ॥ ८ ॥

saukṣmyāt-tadanupalabdhiḥ nā-abhāvāt kāryataḥ tadupalabdheḥ ।
mahadādi tat-ca kāryaṃ prakṛtisarūpaṃ virūpaṃ ca ॥

**– 8 –**

*They (Nature & Spirit) are not perceived due to being subtle,*
*and not because they do not exist.*
*since their effect – intellect, etc. – are seen.*
*(therefore their cause does exist).*
*Effects are similar and also different in nature to their cause.*

Nature and Spirit are said to exist, yet they are not perceived due to conditioning of some sort. What is that conditioning? Furthermore, how can we come to a conclusion about the existence of Nature and Spirit?

Nature and Spirit are very subtle and thus not perceived by the senses. They transcend the human ability to perceive them through direct perception. We can, however, reasonably infer their existence by observing their effects, similar to how a doctor can diagnose an illness and conclude its cause (bacterial or viral infection, etc.) by inference.

There is a universal rule – *"Cause is always more subtle than its effects"*. Clay particles (dust as causal) responsible for a clay pot (pot as effect) are more subtle than the physical pot itself. Gold is simple, but ornaments made by it can be very complex. Similarly, the *Primordial Cause* (pradhāna) – the supreme cause for Nature and all that it contains – must be very subtle. We can reason *Primordial Cause* by looking at its Collective Effect, the way we can infer small particles by examining a clay pot.

Nature, with its 1 intellect, 1 ego, 1 mind, 5 potentialities, 5 sense organs, 5 organs of action, and 5 elements collectively exists. Therefore, their cause must also exist. Without a *Primordial Cause*, these as a collective *effect* cannot exist. This reasoning is why we can infer the existence of a *Primordial Cause* (pradhāna).

Nature as a whole (characterized by its 24 aspects) is similar to its cause, yet different from it, much the same way a child is like its parents in some ways, yet is also different from its parents in other aspects.

### *Points for Reflection*

- Chapter 1 teaches an overview of Sāṅkhya's conceptual model. Knowledge of this model allows the student to accurately discern, differentiate, or discriminate between Nature (Prakṛti/not-Self) and Spirit (Puruṣa/true-Self).
- Chapter 2 introduces logical inquiry as the way to gain the two types of knowledge.
- Passages 4 thru 6 teach Sāṅkhya's technique of logical inquiry and theory of knowledge – of which there are two types.
- The first type of knowledge is a clear intellectual understanding, or its mature form of firm intellectual conviction based on reasoned proof by a valid means of investigation.
- The second type of knowledge was introduced in passage 2, which is liberating knowledge, the type of deep intuitive knowledge that prepares the seeker for that final breakthrough, sometimes called "realization" where the intellectual knowledge matures and shifts, either gradually or suddenly, to the direct realization of the Truth of Self.

# 3
# Causality and the 3 Qualities

असदकरणादुपादानग्रहणात् सर्वसम्भवाऽभावात् ।
शक्तस्य शक्यकरणात् कारणभावाच्च सत्कार्यम् ॥ ९॥

asat-akaraṇāt-upādãnagrahaṇāt sarva-saṃbhavā-abhāvāt ।
śaktasya śakyakaraṇāt kāraṇabhāvāt-ca satkāryam ॥

– 9 –

*Non existing things are not perceived (having utility),*
*suitable material cause is needed (for desired effect),*
*not everything can be caused by everything,*
*a cause with appropriate potential is needed for an effect,*
*an effect is of similar nature to its cause. Due to these reasons,*
*the doctrine of prior existence of an effect in its cause is accepted here.*

Some thinkers claim that everything is born out of nothing. The implication is that if nothing is the cause for everything, then, in essence, everything is indeed nothing. Others believe that creation is born out of something, but effects do not exist prior to manifesting – meaning that non-existing things are born out of existing things. In both cases, effects have no existence before they are created. Therefore, a question is asked here:

Do effects (like intellect, ego, mind, etc.) or any of the 24 principles pre-exist in the cause, or don't they? This question is like asking whether a tree pre-exists in the seed or not. If effects pre-exist in the cause, they cannot be termed non-existing. If the effects do not pre-exist in the cause, they cannot be termed existing. Existence and non-existence (of the same object) are contradictory. Therefore, Sāṅkhya philosophy accepts the doctrine of the pre-existence of effect in its cause. The reasoning can be enumerated as follows:

1. ***Functional instrumentality of non-existing things has never been seen***. Only existing things have utility. (Example: we cannot extract oil from a source in which it does not exist. It can only be extracted from a source where it already exists.) Therefore, for each effect, pre-existence in its cause is accepted by Sāṅkhya.

2. ***Suitable material cause is needed to create an object***. If we want to create a pot, we need clay as material cause. We cannot create a pot from unsuitable materials, clay being a suitable material. This means the pot exists *'in-potentia'* in the clay even before its creation. Since it already exists in its cause, the pot is only an effect, expression, or manifestation of clay. In this way, all the effects of nature, all creation, already exists in its cause in unmanifest form, it only became manifest.

3. ***The effect must pre-exist in its cause.*** If an effect pre-exists in its cause, can the cause be just anything? Not everything can be created from just anything. (Example: A pot's functional potentiality pre-exists in clay more so than cotton or many other materials. Gold cannot become manifest from silver or iron ore, etc.)

4. ***A cause with appropriate potential is needed for an effect.*** Continuing with the clay/pot analogy, clay has the potential to become a functional pot. If we want to make a pot, we must find a form of clay possessing good potential. We cannot create a pot from something that does not have this potential in it, such as silk or cotton. This reinforces Sāṅkhya's acceptance of the pre-existence of effect in its cause.

5. ***An effect is of similar nature to its cause.*** Barley comes from barley seeds and mangoes from mango trees. Today we might say that humans come from human DNA and not, for example from another species specifically. Effect, even as potentiality, must exist in its cause before its creation, expression, or manifestation.

By clear logical reasoning, the effect (such as body, mind, intellect, ego, etc.) pre-exist in its cause as potential in unmanifest form. This is what is meant by the term 'unmanifest' in Sāṅkhya.

# 3 – CAUSALITY AND THE 3 QUALITIES

हेतुमदनित्यमव्यापि सक्रियमनेकमाश्रितं लिङ्गम् ।
सावयवं परतन्त्रं व्यक्तं विपरीतमव्यक्तम् ॥ १० ॥

hetumat-anityam-avyāpi sakriyam-anekam-āśritaṃ liṅgam ।
sāvayavaṃ paratantraṃ vyaktaṃ viparītam-avyaktam ॥

– 10 –

*These are the qualities of the manifest – having a cause, impermanent, limited (non-pervading), active, multiplistic, interdependent, subject to dissolution (destruction), composed of parts, subservient. On other hand, the unmanifest (primordial cause) is of the opposite to these qualities.*

In passage 8, we learned that effects are similar yet also different from their cause. Effects in Nature are called *'manifest'* where as cause in Nature is called *'unmanifest'*. This stanza addresses the differences between the one unmanifest *Primordial Cause* and its various manifest effects. We explain the qualities of manifest Nature first so it will be easier to understand unmanifest Nature later:

1. ***Having a cause*:** An effect cannot exist without its cause. Without a cause, an effect cannot take place. Without clay, we cannot manifest a clay pot. The *Primordial Cause* (Pradhāna) is the cause for intellect. Intellect is the cause for ego. Ego is the cause for the five potentials of variation, and also for the ten organs and the mind. The five potentials for variation are the cause for the five elements – space, air, fire, water, and earth. All of these 23 manifest principles have a cause.

2. ***Impermanent / ever-changing*:** anything that is born out of something other than itself is impermanent and thus, subject to continuous change (Example: the pot has a very short lifespan in comparison with clay. The pot can change, wear out, break, etc. whereas clay remains clay throughout.)

3. ***Limited***: Any effect is more limited than its cause. (Example: Clay is more pervading than a pot. Clay can be anywhere where there is no pot, but a pot cannot be everywhere where clay is found. In other words, clay was there even before the creation of the pot and it will be still there after the pot is broken. The pot has a limited existence.) *Primordial Cause* (Pradhāna) and Spirit (Puruṣa) are all-pervasive, unlike all of their manifest effects.

4. ***Active***: Effects are active, useful, and serve a function. (Example: a pot is actively useful and functional. A pot in its manifest form can be used for various purposes that clay alone as the unmanifest cannot.)

5. ***Multiplistic***: Effects are many, but ultimately their cause is one. (Example: a variety of pots can be created from very same clay. Many different ornament and jewelry can be made out of one lump of gold.)

6. ***Interdependent***: Each effect depends on its cause for its own existence. Without the cause, it cannot exist. (Example: a clay pot depends on clay for its existence. Without clay, a clay pot cannot exist.)

7. ***Subject to dissolution***: An effect, when it is destroyed, it goes back into its cause. (Example: when a pot is broken, it simply reverts to the clay from which it was formed. When a ring is melted at high temperature, it returns molten gold from which it was originally formed.)

8. ***Composed of parts***: Each effect is composed of parts, unlike its cause. (Example: clay is without parts in the sense that it is homogenous, whereas a pot has many different parts – i.e., front, back, upper part, lower part, neck, belly, base, etc.)

9. ***Subservient / not independent***: Since an effect depends on its cause for its own existence, it is not independent. The intellect depends on *Primordial Cause* for its existence. Ego depends on the intellect. Potentiality, organs of action, senses, and mind all depend on ego.

The manifest has been explained and, under inquiry, can be seen as having these qualities. The body-mind organism is the most immediate and intimate example of the manifest. Meaningful inquiry reveals that our sense of self is, and has been, identified with the manifest for most of our lives. Once we clearly understand the manifest, we can realize the unmanifest as having qualities different from the manifest:

1. ***Causeless***: Only effects have a cause, but the Primordial Cause does not have a cause of its own. Primordial Cause is not the creation or result of anything.
2. ***Permanent***: The Primordial Cause is not born out of anything; therefore, it is permanent and eternal. Only something that has a birth can also have death. Primordial Cause is birthless; therefore, it is permanent and timeless.
3. ***All-pervading***: Primordial Cause is all-pervading since it is not limited by time and space (time and space are the creation, the collective effect, of Primordial Cause).
4. ***Inactive***: Something that is all-pervasive and timeless cannot have any motion. Action can take place only in a limited entity.
5. ***One***: Effects are many but their Primordial Cause is only one. Everything – from the intellect, to the ego, to the five elements that make up the universe – is each an effect of the one Primordial Cause.
6. ***Independent***: The Primordial Cause does not depend on anything for its existence therefor it is independent.
7. ***Free from dissolution***: The Primordial Cause has no end, no death, or destruction because it is eternal, all pervasive, and timeless.
8. ***Without parts***: The Primordial Cause is without parts, because only an effect can have parts. The Primordial Cause is not an effect of anything; therefore, it is part-less.
9. ***Free / independent***: The Primordial Cause is not born out of anything, is self-existent, and therefore it is independent and free from being conditioned by another cause.

त्रिगुणमविवेकि विषयः सामान्यमचेतनं प्रसवधर्मि ।
व्यक्तं तथा प्रधानं तद्विपरीतस्तथा च पुमान् ॥ ११ ॥

triguṇam-aviveki viṣayaḥ sāmānyam-acetanaṃ prasavadharmi ।
vyaktaṃ tathā pradhānaṃ tadviparitaḥ tathā ca pumān ॥

ॐ – 11 – ॐ

*The manifest and unmanifest have these similarities: They (1) consist of 3 guṇas, (2) are indiscriminable, (3) objects of perception, (4) common to all, (5) without consciousness, and (6) subject to change. Spirit on other hand is free of these qualities yet it is similar to the unmanifest in some other aspects.*

After examining the differences between manifest and unmanifest Nature, we can look into the similarities between them here:

1. ***They both consist of the 3 qualities (guṇas)***: The manifest (effects, such as the intellect, ego, etc.) as well as unmanifest Primordial Cause both consist of three qualities of energetic equilibrium. In unmanifest Nature, these qualities are in a state of perfect equilibrium, whereas in manifest Nature they are in different ever-fluctuation ratios.

2. ***They both are indiscriminable***: Manifest and unmanifest Nature are not discriminable from qualities, meaning they cannot be understood separately, similar to the way fire and heat is indiscriminable.

3. ***They both are objects of perception***: Manifest and unmanifest Nature are illumined/perceived by Spirit in much the same way that both clay and pot are seen by a person.

4. ***They both are common/general to all***: Manifest and unmanifest Nature are common to all beings. They are perceived and enjoyed by all beings, just as an object such as a pot is seen by many people. The perception of an object is common because it is shared by many beings.

5. ***They both are without consciousness***: Manifest and unmanifest – as cause (material cause like clay) and effect – are both inert. Each is not capable of knowing itself nor the other.

6. ***They both are subject to change***: Manifest (intellect, ego, mind, etc.) are constantly changing. Unmanifest is also ever changing because it is giving birth to the manifest, meaning they both are subject to change.

Spirit on the other hand, is free from these three qualities (sāttva, rājas, and tamās) and their effects. Spirit is separate from everything else. Spirit is not an object of perception or awareness. Spirit is pure Awareness itself, the seer of everything, also known as witness-Consciousness. Unlike manifest and unmanifest Nature, Spirit is not experienced by anything but itself – it is self-evident.

Spirit is not an inert entity but rather is the illuminator of everything. Spirit is of the nature of pure-Consciousness. Because of association with Spirit, intellect, ego, and mind appear animated/sentient. However, without this association, they are inert.

There are some similarities between unmanifest Nature and spirit. In an earlier passage, we learned that *Primordial Cause* differs from its effects. Spirit is also similar to *Primordial Cause* in the following ways:

1. Spirit does not have a cause for its creation.
2. Spirit is permanent and eternal.
3. Spirit is all pervading and timeless.
4. Spirit is inactive; there is no motion or action in Spirit.
5. Universal Spirit is not separate or divided from individualized spirits, meaning they are of same nature.
6. Spirit is independent; it does not depend on anything for its existence.
7. Spirit is free from death, dissolution, or destruction.
8. Spirit is also part-less like unmanifest Nature.
9. Spirit is free from cause-effect conditioning.

प्रीत्यप्रीतिविषादात्मकाः प्रकाशप्रवृत्तिनियमार्थाः ।
अन्योऽन्याभिभवाऽऽश्रयजननमिथुनवृत्तयश्च गुणाः ॥ १२ ॥
prīti-aprīti-viṣāda-ātmakāḥ prakāśa-pravṛtti-niyamārthāḥ ।
anyonya-abhibhava-āśraya-janana-mithuna-vṛttayaḥ ca guṇāḥ ॥

– 12 –

*Sāttva is of the nature of joy, rājas is of pain and struggle, and tamas is of dullness; they are there for clarity, function and control. Overpowering each other, depending on each other, causal to each other, pair to each other, and mixed up in each other.*

In the previous passage, we examined the similarities between unmanifest Nature and Spirit, the similarities between manifest and unmanifest Nature, and the difference between Nature and Spirit. Manifest and unmanifest Nature possess three qualities in potential and also in expression.

What are those three qualities and what is their nature?

(1) Sāttva is of the nature of joy and happiness, (2) rājas is of the nature of pain and struggle, and (3) tamas is of the nature of dullness and delusion.

1. ***Sāttva is goodness, serenity, harmony***: Pure and clear in nature, knowledge, learning, and understanding is possible because of sāttva, and therefore it is of the nature of joy.
2. ***Rājas is passion, ambition, action***: All physical activities and functioning are possible because of rājas. Rājas is also known as the generator of desires, passion, anger, ambition, and greed, and therefore is of the nature of pain and struggle.
3. ***Tamās is ignorance, inertia, laziness***: Sleep, lethargy, dullness, and ignorance is possible because of tamās, and therefore is of the nature of dullness and delusion.

These three qualities are responsible for overpowering each other like a cosmic game of *rock—paper—scissors* at every level of Nature. When one quality is predominant, it overpowers the other two. When sāttva is predominant, rājas and tamās recede. When rājas is predominant, sāttva and tamās draw back. When tamās is predominant, rājas and sāttva withdraw.

1. ***Interdependent upon each other***: These three qualities are always together. They cannot be separated from each other, much the same way a molecule depends on the combination of other smaller particles to maintain its integrity and equilibrium.
2. ***Causal to each other***: One quality is responsible for the generation of other two, much the same way that generating the head of a coin causes the generation of its tail also.
3. ***Antagonistic to each other***: Because they are pair to each other, they are opponent to each other as well, much the same way that a couple experience both love and strife in their relationship.
4. ***Intermixed with each other***: The three qualities are always intermixed in different ratios. There is no pure sāttva, pure rājas, or pure tamās. One quality is responsible for, and reliant upon, the other two.

सत्त्वं लघु प्रकाशकमिष्टमुपष्टम्भकं चलञ्च रजः ।
गुरु वरणकमेव तमः प्रदीपवच्चाऽर्थतो वृत्तिः ॥ १३ ॥

sattvaṃ laghu prakāśakam-iṣṭam-upaṣṭaṃbhakaṃ calaṃ ca rajaḥ ।
guru varaṇakam-eva tamaḥ pradīpavat-ca-arthataḥ vṛttiḥ ॥

– 13 –

*Sāttva is light, bright, and desired.*
*Motivating, rājas is unsteady. Concealing, tamās is heavy.*
*They all work together as a lamp (flame, oil, and wick)*

There is more to these three qualities:

***Sāttva is light and bright in nature***: When sāttva is predominant, the senses and mind are light and sharp, and sentience and cognition are in a pleasant state of harmony. Sāttva is seen or experienced in the meditative state of absorption. It is a state of peace, harmony, serenity, and joy. Because it is free from inner and outer conflict, we desire it.

***Rājas is motivational and unstable***: When rājas is predominant, there are desires and actions, the arising and subsiding ever-changing nature of which makes it unstable.

***Tamas is concealing and heavy***: When tamās is predominant, there is sleep, lethargy, and dullness. The senses can feel so heavy that they cannot function properly. It is most apparent in states of slumber and laziness.

Sāttva, rājas, and tamās oppose each other yet paradoxically function in harmony with each other much the same way that each component in a clay lamp – flame, oil, and wick – opposes each other. Each of the three has a different quality – the flame is light and bright, oil is unstable, whereas the wick is heavy and dull – yet they all come together for a shared function.

अविवेक्यादेः सिद्धिस्त्रैगुण्यात्तद्विपर्ययाऽभावात् ।
कारणगुणाऽऽत्मकत्वात् कार्यस्याऽव्यक्तमपि सिद्धम् ॥ १४ ॥
avivekyādiḥ siddhaḥ traiguṇyāt-tat-viparyaya-abhāvāt ।
kāraṇa-guṇa-ātmakatvāt-kāryasya-avyaktam-api siddham ॥

ॐ – **14** – ॐ

*Indiscriminable, etc. (from passage 11) are established of manifest and unmanifest by having three qualities, by the absence of exclusion, and by (any) effect having the same nature as its cause.*

Passage 11 mentions that manifest and unmanifest Nature are indiscriminable, objects of perception, general, without consciousness, and subject to change. These qualities are apparent in the manifest, but how can they be understood in the unmanifest?

Those qualities are established in the unmanifest by logic and reasoning:

1. ***By having three qualities***: Sāttva, rājas, and tamās are in Nature in manifest and unmanifest forms. These three primary qualities are responsible for other secondary qualities (such as being indiscriminable, etc.). If the three primary qualities exist in unmanifest potential, then secondary qualities also exist in unmanifest potential.

2. ***By their absence or exclusion***: Where the three primary qualities are absent, other secondary qualities (like being indiscriminable, etc.) are also absent. For example, Spirit is free of the three qualities and also free from any other secondary ones as well. Unmanifest Nature, on the other hand, has these three qualities in-potentia, which means it must also have secondary qualities.

3. ***By the effect having the same nature as its cause***: An effect is simply the visible manifestation of its cause. The qualities of the cause will be in its effect as well. For example, a black garment (effect) is woven from black threads (material cause), each displaying the quality of blackness. A clay pot (effect) is created from clay particles (material cause), each exhibiting the quality of clay. Qualities of manifest Nature (effect) must also be in unmanifest Nature (cause).

By this logical reasoning, we establish that manifest and unmanifest Nature (as cause and effect) share the same qualities, as pointed out in passage 11.

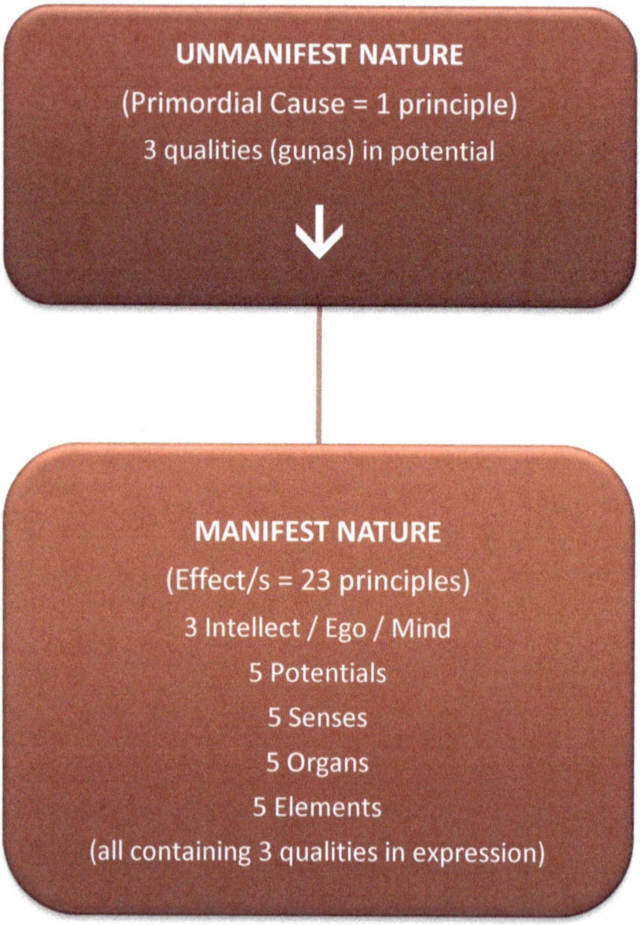
UNMANIFEST NATURE
(Primordial Cause = 1 principle)
3 qualities (guṇas) in potential
MANIFEST NATURE
(Effect/s = 23 principles)
3 Intellect / Ego / Mind
5 Potentials
5 Senses
5 Organs
5 Elements
(all containing 3 qualities in expression)

### *Points for Reflection*

- Sāṅkhya discusses 10 fundamental principles, three of which are presented in Chapter 3.
- Passage 11: **Usefulness of Nature** (Experiences, Liberation, Creation). Nature as a whole is 'useful' in the sense that because of it, creation of the world happens. Nature is 'useful' or in service of Spirit because it provides an instrument through which Spirit experiences the world and itself subjectively. Usefulness in this passage is inferred at this stage of the inquiry.
- Passage 11: **Differentiation between Nature and Spirit**. The result is clear doubt-free understanding of Nature and Spirit, knowledge of which leads to Liberation.
- Passage 14: **Establishment of Primordial Nature** (By Logic). Nature, both manifest and unmanifest, contains the 3 qualities, is ever-changing, and is a collective object to Spirit, the subject.
- The 3 qualities (3 guṇas) are taught as fundamental to all of Nature and its functional processes. Anything, being, or event in the universe, and the universe itself, displaying these qualities belongs to Nature and not Spirit. The 3 qualities each contain elements of each other, they mutually generate and support each other in endless cycles.
- Sāṅkhya's theory of causation is that *"the effect is pre-existent in the cause"*. This is like saying that the entire mango tree is pre-existent in a mango seed, or that all the information for a human being pre-exists in the DNA of an embryo. All of manifest Nature contains the qualities of the *Primordial Cause*, unmanifest Nature.
- Nature as a whole has both unmanifest and manifest forms. The unmanifest is the *Primordial Cause* of the manifest. Unmanifest and manifest are 'cause and effect' and share the same qualities.

# 4
# The Nature of Nature

भेदानां परिमाणात्समन्वयाच्छक्तितः प्रवृत्तेश्च ।
कारणकार्यविभागादविभागाद्वैश्वरूप्यस्य ॥ १५ ॥

bhedānāṃ parimāṇāt samanvayat śaktitaḥ pravṛtteḥ ca ।
kāraṇa-kārya-vibhāgāt-avibhāgāt-vaiśvarūpyasya ॥

ॐ – **15** – ॐ

*(Unmanifest pradhāna is the Primordial Cause of everything because of) effects (parts) being limited/finite, having appropriate connections, activities/functions are possible due to potential power, by the manifestation and dissolution (of effects).*

Passage 14 explains that Nature's manifest expression/s is of the same essence as its unmanifest cause, and that this cause or source is reasoned or understood by understanding the manifest expression/s that we perceive. Just because we don't perceive something doesn't mean it doesn't exist. So many things exist that are imperceptible to human senses. *Primordial Cause* also exists, yet it is not perceived. The reasoning given helps us to infer the existence of a *Primordial Cause*:

1. ***Effects are limited/finite***: Cause is more pervasive than its effect. It is like how clay is more pervasive than a pot made from it. Clay existed before the manifestation of the pot, and it will continue to exist after the destruction of the pot. The pot is also limited to its space, whereas clay exists elsewhere in space where there is no pot. Clay also exists in other items like mug, plate, bowl, etc. A manifest effect is more limited and finite than its cause. Intellect, ego, mind, etc. (effect/s) is finite and limited. There must be a limitless cause from which these effects are born.

2. ***Effects are interconnected***: All the effects (like intellect, ego, mind, etc.) are different and manifold, yet they all are interconnected and share same three qualities (sāttva, rājas, and tamās). This interconnection is possible only if there is a one *Primordial Cause* for all of them having these qualities. Therefore, their *Primordial Cause* does exist. All the gold ornaments such as a crown, ring, bracelet, etc., share the same qualities of gold, therefore gold, as cause must exist.

3. ***Effects' functions are possible because of potential power***: Only a cause with appropriate potential is capable of producing an appropriate effect. Without the presence of potential power, it is not possible to create an effect. Example: a pot is created from clay rather than cotton or silk because clay has the power to fulfill the potential functions of the pot, whereas cotton and silk do not. In similar fashion, a *Primordial Cause* with appropriate potential power does exist and is responsible for the creation of all the effects in Nature (including intellect, ego, mind, etc.).

4. ***The division between cause–effect and its manifestation***: Though effect is manifested from its cause, it is separate from the cause. Example: a pot (effect) can hold any liquid, but clay (cause) cannot. A lump of clay is the material cause of the pot, but a clay lump cannot be created from a pot. They are distinct from each other. There is prior-existence of effect in its cause. Without the cause, the effect cannot exist. An existing effect cannot be born out of non-existing entity. Only an existing entity is manifested from its cause (like oil from seeds), therefore the *Primordial Cause* must exist.

5. ***The dissolution of an effect back into its cause***: Effects are born out of a cause and when they come to an end, they dissolve back into their material cause. An existing entity does not go out of existence; it simply becomes unavailable to perception by dissolving back into its cause. The material cause of humans is a composition of material elements. At death, we decompose back into those same elements.

कारणमस्त्यव्यक्तं प्रवर्तते त्रिगुणतः समुदयाच्च ।
परिणामतः सलिलवत्प्रतिप्रतिगुणाश्रयविशेषात् ॥ १६ ॥

kāraṇam-asti-avyaktaṃ pravartate triguṇataḥ samdayāt-ca ।
pariṇāmataḥ salilavat prati-prati-guṇa-āśraya-viśeṣāt ॥

**– 16 –**

*Unmanifest exists as a cause (for everything) because (effects) operate by three qualities, aggregation, and by transformation like water changes into variety of flavors according to different objects.*

Unmanifest Nature exists as the cause for everything. It is the energetic equilibrium of the 3 qualities and all effects (intellect, ego, mind, etc.) function because of these 3 qualities. These 3 qualities are responsible for the creation of everything. They come together in different combinations to give birth to a result in the same way that a combination of threads results in a fabric. By the various combinations of the 3 qualities, the manifest world is born.

**Q**: If there is only one *Primordial Cause* (pradhāna) for everything, then shouldn't all effects be homogeneous?

**A**: There is variety and differences in effects because of transformation, similar to the way liquid changes in flavor by transformation. Water extracted from coconut and sugarcane is sweet; from lemons and limes, it is sour.

Just because something is born from the same material-cause, does not necessarily mean the effect has to be similar in nature. Body parts are created by living cells yet they each have different functions and qualities.

Where sāttva is predominant, those beings have more clarity and joy. Where rājas is predominant there is more activity and frustration, such as with animal and human lifeforms. Where tamās is predominant, there is dullness and ignorance such as with plant and other lower sentient lifeforms.

Unmanifest Nature does exist as the *Primordial Cause* for everything.

### *Points for Reflection*

- Passage 15 establishes another fundamental principle of Sāṅkhya
- Passage 15: **The Oneness of Nature** (There is only One Nature). Unmanifest (cause) and manifest (effect) Nature are really a single evolving cyclic Nature. Nature, with all its change, cycles, and motion is completely interconnected and unified as One. Since anything in the universe is an effect, we can say it is a Natural effect. If the effect is natural, its cause must also be Natural.
- Both manifest and unmanifest, cause and effect, have 3 qualities (3 guṇas). There are 3 qualities in any potentiality and 3 qualities in any eventuality or expression in Nature. The unmanifest Nature is the functioning power or *Primordial Cause* responsible for the continuous change in everything, being, and event in the universe.
- The 3 qualities in manifest Nature are responsible for the individual differences between beings, things, and events yet all differences and varieties derive from the same *Primordial Cause*.
- If it is difficult to understand the Oneness of Nature, think in terms of an interconnectedness, interrelatedness, or interdependent all-embracing relationship between all beings, things, and events in the universe.

# 5
# The Nature of Spirit

सङ्घातपरार्थत्वात् त्रिगुणादिविपर्ययादधिष्ठानात् ।
पुरुषोऽस्ति भोक्तृभावात् कैवल्यार्थं प्रवृत्तेश्च ॥ १७ ॥

saṅghāta-parārthatvāt triguṇādi-viparyāt-adhiṣṭhānāt ।
puruṣaḥ asti bhoktṛbhāvāt kaivalyārthaṃ pravṛtteḥ ca ॥

ॐ – 17 – ॐ

*Spirit exists because – assembly being for the sake of other,*
*by the absence of 3 qualities, by being a controller,*
*by being experiencer, and by activities*
*being devoted to Liberation (Freedom).*

In the previous two sections, reasoning was used to demonstrate the existence of the unmanifest; now, reasoning is used to establish the existence of spirit in this passage.

It was stated in passage 2 that the understanding of manifest Nature, unmanifest Nature, and Spirit is required to overcome suffering. Because manifest and unmanifest Nature have already been explained, Spirit is now being discussed.

Spirit exists as a separate entity from manifest and unmanifest Nature for the following reasons:

1. ***Assembly being for the sake of other***: Any assembly with its function is there for someone who is not the part of assembly, like a car being there for the sake of a person that is not a car. Car as an assembly means it is made of many different parts, like wheels, engine, doors, etc. This assembly is there not for the car's own sake, but for the sake of a person. Similarly, the intellect, ego, mind, senses, and body are an

assembly – an organism composed of organized parts. It exists not for its own sake, but for the sake of Spirit, which is not the part of assembly. Without the presence of Spirit, this assembly – this body-mind organism – serves no purpose of its own, therefore Spirit exists.

2. ***By the absence of 3 qualitie***s: It was explained in passage 11 that manifest and unmanifest Nature, consisting of the 3 guṇas, have the following qualities: indiscriminable, object of perception, common to all, without consciousness, and subject to change. However, because spirit is devoid of these characteristics, it exists as a distinct entity.

3. ***By being a controller***: Any assembly function is controlled by a sentient being, similar to how a car functions when controlled by a driver. Any assemblage made up of several parts is naturally inert and cannot work independently. Because both manifest and unmanifest Nature are inert, they cannot work independently; therefore, Spirit is their controller.

4. ***By being experiencer***: Because manifest and unmanifest Nature are inert and composed of numerous components, they cannot experience themselves, just as a vehicle composed of many parts cannot experience/enjoy itself. It can only be experienced by a driver who is different from this assembly and also the controller of it; there is a Spirit that is the experiencer of manifest and unmanifest Nature; so, there is a Spirit that exists independent of them.

5. ***By actions being devoted to Liberation***: Manifest and unmanifest Nature is characterized by the cyclical flow or course of all existence (saṃsāra), which means it is constantly changing and giving birth to the pleasure and pain cycle repeatedly. All beings want to be free from suffering. Everyone seeks relief from pain and distress through various activities. If there were no Spirit other than manifest and unmanifest Nature, the struggle for freedom would be meaningless. As a result, Spirit exists apart from manifest and unmanifest Nature.

जन्ममरणकरणानां प्रतिनियमादयुगपत्प्रवृत्तेश्च ।
पुरुषबहुत्वं सिद्धं त्रैगुण्यविपर्ययाच्चैव ॥ १८ ॥

janana-maraṇa-karaṇānāṃ pratininyamāt-ayugapat-pravṛtteḥ ca ।
puruṣa-bahutvaṃ siddhaṃ traiguṇya-viparyayāt-ca-eva ॥

ॐ – 18 – ॐ

*Multiplicity of Spirit is established*
*by specific regulation of birth, death and instrumentality,*[9]
*non-simultaneous function,*
*and by the variation of the 3 qualities.*

Now that we understand that Spirit exists distinct from manifest and unmanifest Nature, we can question whether that Spirit is one or many. Simply put, this passage asserts that each being has his/her own Spirit, appearing as though independent and apart from other beings. This notion is called *'multiplicity of Spirit'*. In this sense, the Spirit that is expressing or manifesting through the body-mind instrument is best understood as witness-Consciousness. Each individual body-mind instrument is illumined and is experiencing by the power of witness-Consciousness – by Spirit (Puruṣa).

Because of the following reasoning, the multiplicity of Spirit is accepted here:

1. ***Specific regulation of birth, death, and instrumentality***: If there was only one spirit, everyone should have been born with the birth of one individual. Everyone should have died if that one person died, and everyone should have been blinded if that one being became blind, but that is not the case. As a result, the multiplicity of spirit is accepted here.

2. ***Non-simultaneous function***: Beings/people engage in a variety of activities. Everyone is involved in various activities; some are

---

[9] *'Instrumentality'* in this context means *'instruments of action, sentience, and cognition'*. We can also think of the body-mind organism as a single *'instrument of experiencing'*, subject to life-cycles of Nature.

righteous, others are criminals, some are seeking liberation, and others have become addicted to worldly pleasure and suffering. If there was only one spirit, they would all be performing the same function, but that is not the case, hence there are multiple spirits/beings.

3. ***Variation of 3 qualities***: People who are predominated by *goodness* (sāttva) are cheerful and serene; those who are predominated by *passion* (rājas) are hyperactive and frustrated; and those who are predominated by *lethargy* (tamās) are lazy, dull, and deluded. This variance is impossible without the multiplicity of spirits, hence it is established that there are many spirits.

Some nondual philosophers consider that there is only one Spirit and that variations in birth, death, activities, and attributes may be resolved simply by discernment or understanding the ever-changing nature of the instrument. Consider how a single sun can be reflected by several mirrors. The sun does not become many as a result of the multiplicity of mirrors. The sun is neither born nor dies as a result of the birth and death of a few mirrors. The sun does not turn colorful as a result of the diverse colors of the mirrors.

It makes no difference whether there is one Spirit or many for the individual who is solely interested in overcoming all suffering. Both schools of thought agree that a proper understanding of Self and not-Self is required for freedom. Self is realized to be free from both manifest and unmanifest Nature. The true source of all suffering is the mistaken identity between Self and not-Self, and by removing that false identification, one can realize freedom from all suffering.

A person imprisoned in a jail is concerned only with his or her own freedom, not if there are many other prisoners in that jail, or if they are the only one. Even if others are present, initial freedom for the first person is required in order to aid others. In this case, the goal is freedom rather than a conceptual model or philosophical argument. In both circumstances, Spirit is the true-Self's identity.

## 5 – THE NATURE OF SPIRIT

तस्माच्च विपर्यासात्सिद्धं साक्षित्वमस्य पुरुषस्य ।
कैवल्यं माध्यस्थ्यं द्रष्टृत्वमकर्त्तृभावश्च ॥ १९ ॥

tasmāt-ca viparyāsāt siddhaṃ sākṣitvam-asya puruṣasya ।
kaivalyaṃ mādhyastyaṃ draṣṭṛtvam-akartṛbhāvaḥ ca ॥

ॐ **– 19 –** ॐ

*Therefore, by being different (from manifest and unmanifest Nature) it is established that Spirit is witness-Consciousness, ever free, impartial, spectator, and non-doer.*

In passage 11, it is stated that Spirit is distinct from manifest and unmanifest Nature and its attributes. Spirit is free of the three characteristics (sāttva, rājas, tamās) and their effects. Spirit is distinct from everything else. It is never an object of Awareness; it is the seer of everything. Because Spirit is distinct from all of Nature and its characteristics, we can infer that Spirit is witness-Consciousness, as all change, transformation, and activity occur in both manifest and unmanifest Nature. Spirit is unchanging Consciousness that observes all activities and changes. Qualities attract (ego) into actions, whereas witness-Consciousness neither attracts nor repels.

Because Spirit is witness-Consciousness, it is also detached from manifest and unmanifest Nature; it is impartial, like a judge who does not favor one side or the other. A spectator, like a moviegoer, is unaffected by the good and bad happening in the show or onscreen. Doership takes place in the realm of manifest Nature – in the personal and egoic – rather than in the Spirit. Therefore, witness-Consciousness is not a doer of anything.

### *Points for Reflection*

- Passages 17, 18, and 19 establish three additional fundamental principles of Sāṅkhya
- Passage 17: **Nature is an 'Object of Experience' in Service of Spirit.** Nature allows for Spirit to experience the world, the body-mind and itself subjectively. Investigation into Nature and Spirit leads to intellectual or conceptual Self-knowledge. Whether naturally, or through effort and discipline of spiritual practices such as concentration and absorption, the conceptual knowledge of Nature deepens and matures until Nature and Spirit are fully realized.
- Passage 18: **Multiplicity of Intellects and Spirits**. Sāṅkhya philosophy and its technique of inquiry is primarily concerned with the Self as it applies to the individual. From the personal perspective, the Truth of Self is pure-Spirit embodied in each individual. Sāṅkhya accepts that there are many bodies, guided by many intellects and also many Spirits.
- Passage 19: **Inactiveness of Spirit**. Sāṅkhya teaches that Spirit is witness-Consciousness, the Awareness behind all experiencing, but that it is never the doer or controller of anything. Unmanifest Nature, the *Primordial Cause*, is causal to all universal activity. Spirit and unmanifest Nature are similar, but not to be confused as the same.

# 6

# Yoga: Divine-Union

तस्मात्तत्संयोगादचेतनं चेतनावदिव लिङ्गम् ।
गुणकर्तृत्वे च तथा कर्तेव भवत्युदासीनः ॥ २० ॥

tasmāt-tat-saṃyogāt-acetanaṃ cetanāvat-iva liṅgam ।
guṇakartṛtve-api tathā karteva bhavati-udāsīnaḥ ॥

ॐ – 20 – ॐ

*Therefore, indicators[10] appear as sentient by the association with Spirit; indifferent Spirit also appears as the doer by association of activities of qualities (3 guṇas).*

If Spirit is distinct from them, how can this cognition occur - I will do good deeds and refrain from doing bad ones? If the mind is inert and the Spirit is not a doer, experiencing will not happen, but this is not the case. As a result of their association with Spirit, mind, intellect, ego, and so forth appear sentient even though they are inert by nature. This appearance by association is analogous to how a red-hot iron rod temporarily appears bright and hot due to its relationship with fire, even though it is neither hot nor bright by nature.

Similarly, by associating with attributes (sāttva, rājas, tamās and their products), indifferent Spirit appears to be the doer. This means that the indifferent Spirit manifests itself in a multitude of ways. Spirit appears as the thinker due to its association with intellect. Spirit, when associated with the ego, seems as the doer. Spirit, when associated with the mind, appears both joyful and sad. Spirit seems to be sentient (seer, listener, etc.) because it is associated with the senses. All of these actions and attributes have to do with qualities (3 guṇas) and not the Spirit, although these qualities are

---

[10] indicators = intellect, ego, mind, senses

superimposed onto indifferent Spirit. This is analogous to how an innocent person found in the company of criminals is likewise labeled a criminal by association. Spirit is not the doer of actions. Spirit (Puruṣa) is indifferent. It doesn't do any action nor does it judge, but rather is witness-Consciousness and just observes. It is Awareness. Spirit (Puruṣa), when associated with Nature in the form of the body-mind instrument and the three energetic qualities of Nature, merely appears as though it is the doer.

पुरुषस्य दर्शनार्थं कैवल्यार्थं तथा प्रधानस्य ।
पङ्गवन्धवदुभयोरपि संयोगस्तत्कृतः सर्गः ॥ २१ ॥

puruṣasya darśanārthaṃ kaivalyārthaṃ tathā pradhānasya ।
paṅgu-andhavat-ubhayoḥ api saṃyogaḥ tat-kṛtaḥ sargaḥ ॥

ॐ – **21** – ॐ

*Association is there for the Liberation of Spirit*
*and for the experience of Nature*
*like the association of a blind and crippled,*
*the creation is the product of association.*

When two things work together (association), there must be some utility. It is a universal law that two distinct things will never cooperate if utility and outcome are not present. So, what's the point of this?

The association between Spirit and Nature is beneficial to both parties. Spirit cannot realize its true immortal, unchanging nature unless Nature is present. Nature cannot be experienced without the presence of Spirit, just as a person cannot see their face without a mirror.

The union of Spirit and Nature (Puruṣa and Prakṛti) is compared to a blind person carrying a lame person on their back. The blind person is able to walk but cannot see. As a result, he is unable to navigate. A lame person, on the other hand, is able to see but unable to walk. The two collaborate by the lame person climbing onto the blind person's shoulders and offering guidance so that they can both go forward. The blind person does all of the labor, while the lame person sees everything. Nature, like the blind man, is capable of movement but not vision. Nature is blind, meaning mechanistic, systematic, and subject to cause and effect in its doing. Spirit is like a lame person. It can see but cannot move. Spirit is a non-doer, yet it is pure Awareness, seeing everything. Nature and spirit complement one another. The creation is the outcome of their association. However, they must be clearly differentiated in order to understand Nature and Spirit.

### *Points for Reflection*

- Passages 20 and 21 establish two additional fundamental principles of Sāṅkhya.
- Passage 20: **Separation of Spirit from Nature = Liberation**. Liberation means Spirit free and distinct from Nature. Spiritual Liberation describes knowing one's true identity as pure-Spirit alone. The Self as Spirit uses Nature or the not-Self as instruments of experiencing, but is and always has been ever free and unattached to Nature.
- Passage 21: **Confusion between Spirit and Nature = Bondage**. Bondage simply means that we feel bound and limited by the natural limitations of the body-mind organism and Nature in general. The feeling of being bound and limited is due to ignorance and error regarding our true identity as pure-Spirit. As long as we think we are a product of, or an 'object' in Nature, we are not free (Liberated) from this false idea, this false identification – we are not yet free from ignorance and error. Sprit (Self) experiences Nature (not-Self) as undifferentiated, and we feel bound due to confusion between Self and not-Self.

# 7
# Emergent Principles

प्रकृतेर्महांस्ततोऽहङ्कारस्तस्माद्गणश्च षोडशकः ।
तस्मादपि षोडशकात्पञ्चभ्यः पञ्च भूतानि ॥ २२ ॥

prakṛteḥ mahāṃ tataḥ ahaṃkāraḥ tasmāt-gaṇaḥ ca śoḍaśakaḥ ।
tasmāt-api ṣoḍaśakāḥ pañcabhyaḥ pañcabhūtāni ॥

– 22 –

*From the unmanifest, intellect is born,*
*from intellect comes ego,*
*from ego comes 16 elements,*
*and 5 gross elements come from 5 subtle elements.*

In a previous section, it is said that creation is the result of a relationship between Spirit and Nature, similar to how a male-female relationship results in the birth of a child.

It was explained in passage 2 that freedom from suffering can be realized through a correct understanding of manifest and unmanifest Nature and Spirit. Their existence can be established by logical reasoning, and they are currently being investigated in greater depth.

Nature (Prakṛti/Pradhāna) is also known as the *Primordial Cause*, the unmanifest (avyakta), and Illusion (māyā). Manifest instruments and elements emerge from unmanifest Nature.

Intellect (mahat) is also known as buddhi-intelligence (buddhi), cognition (mati), knowledge (khyāti), etc. Ego as the 'I-sense' – the feeling of being an individual – arises from the intellect.

The ego gives rise to 16 other elements: 5 potentials + 5 senses of knowledge + 5 action organs + 1 mind.[11] From 5 potentials emerge 5 gross elements: space from sound potential, air from touch potential, fire from sight potential, water from taste potential, and earth from smell potential.

अध्यवसायो बुद्धिर्धर्मो ज्ञानं विरागं ऐश्वर्यम् ।
सात्विकमेतद्रूपं तामसमस्माद्विपर्यस्तम् ॥ २३ ॥

adhyavasāyaḥ buddhiḥ dharmaḥ jñānaṃ virāga aiśvaryam ।
sāttvikam-etad-rūpaṃ tāmasam-asmāt-viparyastam ॥

– 23 –

*Intellect is ascertainment.*
*Virtue, knowledge, dispassion, and mastery*
*are qualities of sāttvic intellect;*
*qualities of tamāsic intellect are opposite to them.*

It was previously stated that cognition is born from the unmanifest. What is its distinguishing characteristic?

Intellect is the power of ascertainment and apprehension; it is responsible for cognition and comprehension. It can be divided into 8 parts through the division of sāttva and tamas.

Sāttva contains four components: virtue, knowledge, dispassion, and mastery.

1. ***Virtues*** are yama, niyama etc. they are well listed in the *Yoga Sutras* of Patañjali.

---

[11] In the western context, the word 'mind' is used in a general sense. The Sanskrit translation for 'mind' in *general* sense is 'inner-instrument'. In Sāṅkhya, the 'inner-instrument' means the '3-fold mind' because it consists of (1) a questioning 'mind' that feels emotions + (2) a reasoning 'intellect' that thinks thoughts + (3) an 'ego' as self-image or simply the 'I-sense'. In Vedānta, the 'inner-instrument' means the '4-fold mind' consisting of the same as Sāṅkhya, but to which Vedānta adds (4) an active, subconscious, and psychologically conditioned 'memory'. These are interrelated mental functions of the 'inner-instrument'.

अहिंसा-सत्य-अस्तेय-ब्रह्मचर्य-अपरिग्रहाः यमाः। absence of violence, truthfulness, absence of theft, absence of unethical sexual behavior/celibacy, non-possessive attitude are Yama.

शौचसन्तोष-तपः-स्वाध्याय-ईश्वरप्रणिधानानि नियमाः। purity (of body and mind), contentment, penance/hardship, commitment to duty, surrendering to higher power are niyama.

2. ***Knowledge*** is synonymous with understanding. There are two distinct forms: external and internal.

   Scriptures, grammar, astrology, astronomy, history, logic, theology, mythology, math, physics, and all other sciences are examples of external knowledge. All of these disciplines are always only ever concerned with the not-Self.

   Inner knowledge is a clear understanding of Self and not-Self gained by means of Discernment. Nature – the not-Self – is inert. It is the equilibrium of the three characteristics (3-guṇas). Spirit is witness-Consciousness; it is free of all attributes, unattached and unlimited, which means it is ever free, never bound. We may attain wealth, prestige, celebrity, and popularity through exterior knowledge, but only inner-knowledge can lead to spiritual freedom.

3. ***Dispassion*** is of two kinds: inner and external. The absence of longing for worldly items is defined as external. We can achieve this level of dispassion by observing afflictions and the added suffering they produce. We who are purely pursuing liberation can realize inner dispassion when we come to regard everything – including both manifest and unmanifest Nature – as illusory, like objects in a dream.

4. ***Mastery*** refers to eight distinct types of exceptional skills that can be realized by intense focus and concentration, such as the ability to comprehend subtle and invisible things like atoms, frequencies, and so on, as well as the ability to comprehend large things like space, the distance between two stars or planes, and so on. Patañjali's *Yoga Sutras* list and describe these eight categories of powers.

Tamāsic intellect has four aspects that are diametrically opposed to the four parts of Sāttvic intellect: (1) lack of virtue, (2) ignorance, (3) lack of dispassion, and (4) lack of mastery.

अभिमानोऽहङ्कारस्तस्माद् द्विविधः प्रवर्तते सर्गः ।
एकादशकश्च गणस्तन्मात्रपञ्चकश्चैव ॥ २४ ॥

abhimānaḥ ahaṃkāraḥ tasmād dvidhaḥ pravartate sargaḥ ।
ekādāśakaḥ ca gaṇaḥ tanmātraḥ pañcakaḥ ca-eva ॥

**– 24 –**

*Ego is the sense of 'I' (I am an individual),*
*from it, two types of creation are born,*
*a group of 11 organs of senses, and 5 potentials.*

Following the explanation of intellect, ego is described as the sense of 'I'. The ego gives birth to two distinct types of creation: the first is subjective: ego gives rise to a group of 11 sense organs = 5 senses of knowledge + 5 organs of action + 1 mind.[12]

The second is objective: ego gives rise to a group of 5 potentials = sound potential, touch potential, form potential, taste potential, and smell potential.

There are two parts to creation: subject and object. The first group consists of subjects/experiencers, while the second group consists of the objects/experienced. This is the genesis of all creation. Everything is nothing more than the manifestation of the universal ego; the ego generates subject-object duality.

---

[12] In Sāṅkhya, the term *'inner-instrument'* in the general sense is 3-fold, comprised of (1) reasoning intellect, (2) ego as 'I'-sense, and (3) questioning *'mind'* as a function in a specific lower sense of the term.

सात्विक एकादशकः प्रवर्तते वैकृतादहङ्कारात् ।

भूतादेस्तन्मात्रः स तामसस्तैजसादुभयम् ॥ २५ ॥

sāttvikaḥ ekādaśakaḥ pravartate vaikṛtād ahaṃkārāt ।

bhūtādeḥ tanmātraḥ sa tāmasaḥ taijasād ubhayam ॥

– 25 –

*From sāttvic ego, a group of eleven is born,*

*from tamāsic ego, a group of five is born,*

*from rājasic ego both are born.*

According to an earlier passage, two sorts of creation are born from the ego. How can one ego be the source of two distinct creations?

Everything is an expression of a three-quality energetic combination. As a result, those three characteristics exist in everything.

A group of 11 is born from the sāttvic part of the ego. This subject group appears sentient because it is born from sāttva. A set of 5 elemental potentials emerges from the tamāsic part of the ego. Because this object group of potentials is derived from tamās, it appears insentient and inert. Because sāttva is pure and tamās is dull, neither is capable of creating without the assistance of rājas. Both come from rājas, and hence both have actions.

बुद्धीन्द्रियाणि चक्षुःश्रोत्रघ्राणरसनत्वगाख्यानि ।

वाक्पाणिपादपायूपस्थानि कर्मेन्द्रियाण्याहुः ॥ २६ ॥

buddhi-indriyaṇi cakṣuḥ srotra-ghrāṇa-rasana-tvak-ākhyāni ।

vāk-pāṇi-pāda-pāyū-upastāḥ karmendriyāṇi-āhuḥ ॥

– 26 –

*Senses (of perception) are eyes, ears, nose, tongue, and skin,*

*organs (of action) are larynx, hands, legs, anus, and genitals.*

In an earlier section, it is stated that a group of 11 is born from the sāttvic ego; what are they?

The 5 senses of perception are the eyes, ears, nose, tongue, and skin; they receive information from the outside world of objects. The organs of action are the hands (for manipulation), legs (for mobility), larynx (for speech), anus (for waste disposal), and genitals (for reproduction). To the 5 senses of perception (also known as 'organs of knowledge') and the 5 organs of action, we must add the mind to total 11 subjective instruments.

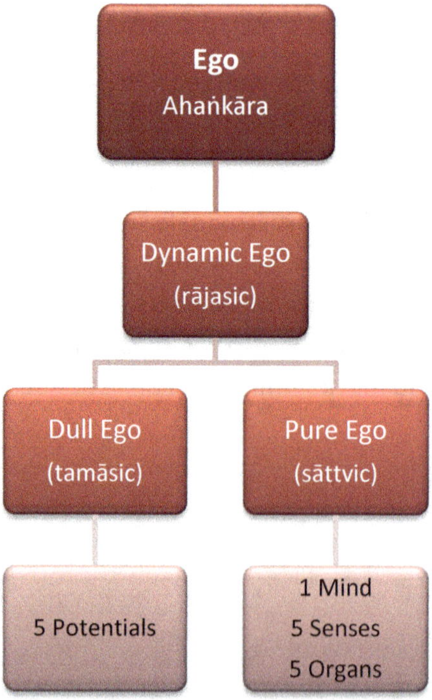

उभयात्मकमत्र मनः सङ्कल्पकमिन्द्रियञ्च साधर्म्यात् ।
गुणपरिणामविशेषान्नानात्वं बाह्यभेदाश्च ॥ २७ ॥

ubhayātmakam-atra manaḥ saṅkalpakam-indriyaṃ ca sādharmyāt ।
guṇa-pariṇāma-viśeṣāt-nānātvaṃ bāhya-bhedāḥ ca ॥

**– 27 –**

*Due to similarities, thinking (desiring) mind is an instrument,*
*and both (instrument of perception and instrument of action),*
*by the differences of qualities and their modifications*
*there is multiplicity and external differences.*

The mind can be understood to be both a sensory organ and an organ of action. The mind also has its own distinct role - thinking. Mind can be considered similar to senses and organs because it emerges from the ego and assists the other two in functioning.

Though these 11 subject instruments are all born from the same ego, they are all born from different combinations of the three qualities (3-guṇas). As a result, these instruments are numerous and distinct from one another.

शब्दादिषु पञ्चानामालोचनमात्रमिष्यते वृत्तिः ।
वचनाऽदानविहरणोत्सर्गाऽनन्दश्च पञ्चानाम् ॥ २८ ॥

śabdadiṣu pañcānām ālocanamātram-iṣyate vṛttiḥ ।
vacana-ādāṇa-viharaṇa-utsarga-ānandāḥ ca pañcānām ॥

**– 28 –**

*Functions of the 5 senses are to perceive sound etc. only.*
*Functions of the 5 organs are*
*speaking, handling, traveling, excretion, and pleasure.*

What are their functions?

The functions of the 5 senses are to perceive their respective objects. Only the eyes can observe forms, only the ears can perceive sound, only the skin can perceive touch, only the tongue can perceive taste, and only the nose can perceive scent.

The function of the larynx is communication, the function of the hands is giving and taking (work), the function of the legs is travel, the function of the anus is excretion (purification), and the function of the genitals is pleasure (reproduction).

स्वालक्षण्यं वृत्तिस्त्रयस्य सैषा भवत्यसामान्या ।
सामान्यकरणवृत्तिः प्राणाद्या वायवः पञ्च ॥ २९ ॥

svālakṣanyaṃ vṛttiḥ trayasya saiṣā bhavati-asāmānya ।
sāmānya-karaṇa-vṛttiḥ prāṇādyā vāyavaḥ pañca ॥

– 29 –

*Specific characteristics are also the peculiar function of the three (intellect, ego, and mind),*
*common functions of all are the five life-forces (prāṇas)*

The functions of the senses and organs were discussed in the previous passages. Mind, intellect, and ego functions are now being explained. The three's defining features (mind, intellect, and ego) are also their functions. Determination is an intellect function, identification is an ego function, and thinking is a mind function.[13]

All 13 (5 senses + 5 organs + 1 mind + 1 intellect + 1 ego) specific functions have been explained, and now all of their common functions are explained. Because life force is shared by all, life force is their shared function. Life force is divided into five parts based on their distinct roles.

[13] Sāṅkhya recognizes intellect, ego, and mind as the three primary functions of the inner-instrument, whereas memory is implied as present in all three functions.

युगपच्चतुष्टयस्य तु वृत्तिः क्रमशश्च तस्य निर्दिष्टा ।
दृष्टे तथाऽप्यदृष्टे त्रयस्य तत्पूर्विका वृत्तिः ॥ ३० ॥

yugapat-catuṣṭayasya tu vṛttiḥ krama-śaśca tasya nirdiṣṭā ।
dṛṣṭe tathā-api-adṛṣṭe trayasya tat-pūrvikā vṛttiḥ ॥

– 30 –

*Function of the four can be simultaneous or sequential,*
*with indirect-perception, only three are functioning,*
*with direct-perception, four are functioning.*

Mind, intellect, ego (cognition), and senses (sentience)[14] all collaborate to grasp external objects and make conclusions. Depending on the circumstances, this process can occur simultaneously or gradually.

**Example 1**: A person in a dark cave sees a tiger in front of him/her due to a flash of lightning in the sky and immediately decides to flee from it.

**Example 2**: A person sees something in the distant at twilight and subsequently concludes that it is a tree trunk rather than a person.

Intellect, ego, mind, and eyes work together to perceive shape, while ears perceive sound, skin perceives touch, the nose perceives aroma, and the tongue perceives taste. We perceive sense-objects by direct perception. Sentience + Cognition is the result of the 4 (intellect, ego, mind, and senses) working together. The waking state is one example of this.

Because the object is an unseen/remote entity, only intellect, ego, and mind are functioning in relation to an indirect object; senses cannot function here. All 4 are active in the context of direct perception of sense-objects. In the case of indirect perception of thought-forms, just the 3 (intellect, ego, mind) are functioning without the senses, relying solely on Cognition. The dream state is one example of this.

---

[14] Instruments of perception – Sentience + Cognition. Here, *'sentience'* = external biodata input through sentience / *'cognition'* = inner biodata processing by intellect, ego, and mind functions.

स्वां स्वां प्रतिपदयन्ते परस्पराऽकूतहेतुकां वृत्तिम् ।
पुरुषार्थ एव हेतुर्न केनचित् कार्यते करणम् ॥ ३१ ॥

svāṃ svāṃ pratipadyante paraspara-ākuta-hetukāṃ vṛttim ।
puruṣārtha eva hetuḥ na kenacit kāryate karaṇam ॥

**– 31 –**

*Instruments perform their respective functions accordingly,*
*they are not forced by anything in their activities,*
*but, for the sake of the Spirits' enjoyment and freedom, they function.*

Instruments such as the intellect, ego, mind, senses, and organs carry out their particular functions such as thinking, knowing, and acting, among others. Nothing forces instruments into their functions, but they are active in their functions to provide enjoyment (pain and pleasure) and Liberation to the Spirit (witness-Consciousness).

करणं त्रयोदशविधं तदाहरणधारणप्रकाशकरम् ।
कार्यं च तस्य दशधाऽऽहार्यं धार्यं प्रकाश्यञ्च ॥ ३२ ॥

karaṇaṃ trayodaśavidhaṃ tat āharaṇa dhāraṇa prakāśakaram ।
kāryaṃ ca tasya daśadha āhāryaṃ dhāryaṃ prakāśyaṃ ca ॥

**– 32 –**

*There are 13 Instruments;*
*receivers, retainers, and knowers.*
*Their functions are receiving, retaining, and knowing.*

There are 13 instruments: three are intellect, ego, and mind, 5 senses, and 5 organs. Organs receive and retain data, whereas senses lead to understanding. They serve ten various purposes. Understanding is comprised of 5 functions: sight, sound, smell, touch, and taste. The five actions are handling, traveling, speaking, excreting, and pleasuring/reproducing.

अन्तःकरणं त्रिविधं दशधा बाह्यं त्रयस्य विषयाख्यम् ।
साम्प्रतकालं बाह्यं त्रिकालमाभ्यन्तरं करणम् ॥ ३३ ॥

antaḥ karaṇaṃ trividhaṃ daśadhā bāhyaṃ trayasya viṣayākhyam ।
sāmpratakālaṃ bāhyaṃ trikālam ābhyantaraṃ karaṇam ॥

**– 33 –**

*There are 3 inner instruments and 10 outer,*
*The outer are governed by the inner.*
*Outer can only perceive the present,*
*inner can perceive past, present, and future.*

Inner instruments are intellect, ego, and mind, whereas outside instruments are the five senses and five organs of action. The outer instruments are governed by the inner instruments, which mean that the outer instruments are objects to the inner instruments, with the inner instruments experiencing and motivating the outer instruments.

Outer instruments, such as the eyes, ears, and so on, can only sense present objects, which means that the eyes can only view objects that are present. It is unable to see items in the past or future. Similarly, the ears can only hear current sound and not future or past sound. The hand can only grasp anything that is current, but it cannot grasp something that is not present, existing only in the past or future. Similarly, all other senses and organs can perceive objects that are currently present now, not those that exist only during the past or future.

Inner instruments, on the other hand, such as intellect, ego, and mind, can perceive items from the past, present, and future. Intellect can comprehend, for example, a pot from the past, present, and future. The ego can identify with the past, the present, and the future. For example, *"I was a child"*, *"I am a person"*, and *"I will be elderly"*. A mind is capable of contemplating the past, present, and future. For instance, *"I desire objects from the previous century"*, *"I desire objects from modern society"*, and *"I desire objects from a future civilization"*.

बुध्दीन्द्रियाणि तेषां पञ्च विशेषाऽविशेषविषयाणि ।
वाग्भवति शब्दविषया शेषाणि तु पञ्चविषयाणि ॥ ३४ ॥

buddhi indriyāṇi teṣāṃ pañca viśeṣa aviśeṣa viṣayāṇi ।
vāk bhavati śabda viṣayā śeṣāṇi tu pañca viṣayāṇi ॥

**– 34 –**

*Among them, Senses perceive their five specific objects,*
*subtle and gross,*
*the larynx producing gross sound, (along with the)*
*others (hands, legs, anus, and genitals), function on the 5-fold objects.*

Of the outer instruments, the senses can perceive both subtle and gross objects (the 5 potentials are subtle objects). The senses of a great yogi can perceive both subtle and gross objects. Ordinary people can only perceive crude sounds, forms, touches, tastes, and odors. Due to their intense focus and practices, yogis have extraordinary sensory capacity and can perceive things that ordinary people cannot. Modern technology can produce the same outcomes, just as a microscope, EKG, MRI, and other innovations like these can assist an ordinary person in seeing things that are not easily visible to the human eye.

Because subtle sound (sound potential) is the result of ego, the sound produced by the larynx is gross, whether produced by an ordinary person or a great yogi. As a result, the larynx can only create gross sounds and not subtle ones.

*"The other four – hands, legs, anus, and genitals – act on the fivefold objects"* refers to objects possessing fivefold characteristics. A hand, for example, can handle an 'object' having touch, form, smell, sound, and taste qualities.

साऽन्तःकरणा बुद्धिः सर्वं विषयमवगाहते यस्मात् ।
तस्मात्त्रिविधं करणं द्वारि द्वाराणि शेषाणि ॥ ३५ ॥

śāntaḥ karaṇaṃ buddhiḥ sarvaṃ viṣayam avagāhate yasmāt ।
tasmāt trividhaṃ karaṇaṃ dvāri dvārāṇi śeṣāṇi ॥

**– 35 –**

*Because the intellect, with the inner instruments (ego and mind), perceive everything, for that reason, the 3 inner instruments are primary and the others are secondary.*

The 3 inner instruments – intellect, ego, and mind – perceive past, present, and future, which means they can perceive everything that exists in any timeframe; thus, they are primary, whereas the other ten (5 senses + 5 organs of action) are secondary because they function only in the present and require support from the primary instrument to function. For example, senses cannot function in the absence of the mind, so a person who is sleeping cannot see or hear anything around them.

एते प्रदीपकल्पाः परस्परविलक्षणा गुणविशेषाः ।
कृत्स्नं पुरुषस्याऽर्थं प्रकाश्य बुद्धौ प्रयच्छन्ति ॥ ३६ ॥

ete pradīpakalphāḥ paraspara vilakṣaṇāḥ guṇa viśeṣāḥ ।
kṛtsaṃ puruṣayā arthaṃ prakāśya buddhau prayacchanti ॥

**– 36 –**

*They work as lamp, different from each other, born out of qualities; they offer / deliver everything to intellect for the sake of spirit.*

They all are unique and evolved from varying combinations of the three qualities, and yet they all function as lamps to reveal their objects. All instruments provide information to intellect for the enjoyment (experience) of Spirit, meaning that this inert assembly (organism) works together for the benefit of sentient Spirit.

सर्वं प्रत्यपभोगं यस्मात् पुरुषस्य साधयति बुद्धिः ।
सैवा च विशिनष्टि पुनः प्रधानपुरुषाऽन्तरं सूक्ष्मम् ॥ ३७ ॥

sarvaṃ prati upabhogaṃ yasmāt puruṣasya sādhayati buddhiḥ ।
sa eva ca viśinaṣṭi punaḥ pradhāna puruṣāṅtaraṃ sūkṣmam ॥

**– 37 –**

*Since intellect accomplishes everything for the Spirit,*
*the intellect also reveals the difference between Spirit and Nature,*
*which is very subtle.*

Inner instruments take precedence over outer instruments. The intellect is the superior inner instrument to the ego and mind. The intellect governs all activity of all the other instruments. The intellect receives all information from various instruments and converts it into helpful information for the enjoyment of the Spirit. When the intellect is influenced by rājas and tamās, it causes suffering and delusion. It reveals the distinction between Spirit (real) and Nature (unreal) when it becomes pure through sāttva. Because both Spirit and Nature are imperceptible to the senses, the differences between them are subtle, but graspable with pure intellect. Moreover, by having a proper understanding of Spirit and Nature, we can overcome the suffering created by ignorance and delusion.

तन्मात्राण्यविशेषास्तेभ्यो भूताणि पञ्च पञ्चभ्यः ।
एते स्मृता विशेषाः शान्ता घोराश्च मूढाश्च ॥ ३८ ॥

tanmātrāṇi aviśeṣāḥ tebhyo bhūtāni pañca pañcabhyaḥ ।
ete smṛtāḥ viśeṣāḥ śāṅtāḥ ghorāḥ ca mūḍhāḥ ca ॥

**– 38 –**

*5 potentials are general,*
*from the 5 general potentials comes 5 specific elements,*
*they are of the nature of joy, suffering, and delusion.*

It was previously stated that ego gives birth to 5 unspecific (subtle) potentials, which give birth to the 5 elements.

Sound potential, touch potential, form potential, taste potential, and smell potential are the five potentials. Space, air, fire, water, and earth emerge from these five potentials.[15] Potential is prior to the actual.

Space is generated from sound potential / air is generated from sound and touch potentials / fire is generated from sound, touch, and form / water is generated from sound, touch, form, and taste potentials / and earth is generated from sound, touch, form, taste, and smell potentials.

They can be a source of joy, suffering, and delusion. For example, space can be a source of comfort and joy for someone who, having been trapped in a restricted environment emerges into a wide-open space. It can be a source of suffering for someone exposed to the elements during oppressive winter cold, torrential rain, or summer heat. It might be a source of delusion for someone who has become disoriented in the forest. Similarly, the other elements can also be sources of joy, suffering, and delusion.

[15] These roughly coincide with modern science's classical low-energy phases or "states of matter", as *solid* (earth), *liquid* (water), *plasma* (fire), and *gas* (air) available to the senses + *other states* (space). Insightful yogis saw, understood, or inferred these thousands of years ago till today.

### *Points for Reflection*

- Passages 23, 45, 65 are the only passages that allude to 'yogic' practices. In Chapter 7, passage 23 focuses on attaining a sāttvic (pure or harmonious) intellect. Yoga as a practice has the aim of us becoming more sāttvic as the primary state or mode of functioning and experiencing. Sāttva is NOT Self-realization or Liberation, but rather is human maturity in its most harmless and beneficial expression.
- Passage 37: **Nature exists for the sake of Spirit**, in service of the Spirit. Nature serves as both a school and playground for the human experience. It guides us either naturally and gently, or through effort and discipline, to a sāttvic and dharmic way of being – beneficial inner intentions and beneficial outer expressions. When we gain inner purity with regard to our intentions, and outer purity with regard to our interactions, we prepare ourselves for Self-realization and Liberation.
- Creation, the entire universe and everything, being, and event in it, is an effect hidden in unmanifest Nature, the *Primordial Cause*. Under the right conditions, all of creation manifests and evolves.
- Nature provides the means and objects for Spirit to see and enjoy Nature. Nature, the world, our living human experience, has a purpose according to Sāṅkhya. The purpose or meaning of life, according to Sāṅkhya philosophy is for Spirit's witnessing and enjoyment. It is as if Spirit gets lost in enjoying the play, but then returns home.
- Nature aids towards Spirit's freedom. The intellect-ego-mind instrument is Nature. This instrument is what feels bound. Nature serves this instrument in the sense that by Nature, we stop ignoring the primary questions concerning bondage, suffering, and identity. When the instrument stops ignoring and begins inquiry into Nature and Spirit, Self and not-Self, it puts an end to the error of misunderstanding and false identity. Spirit is and always has been ever free. The realization of this fact is what is meant by Liberation of the Spirit. Spirit has always been Liberated.

# 8

# The 'Real'

सूक्ष्मा मातापितृजाः सह प्रभूतैस्त्रिधा विशेषाः स्युः ।
सूक्ष्मास्तेषां नियता मातापितृजा निवर्तन्ते ॥ ३९॥

sūkṣmāḥ mātāpitṛjāḥ saha prabhūtaiḥ tridhā viśeṣāḥ syuḥ ।
sūkṣmāḥ teṣāṃ niyatāḥ mātā pitṛjāḥ nivartaṇte ॥

ॐ – 39 – ॐ

*Subtle (bodies), gross bodies that are born from mother and father with gross elements, are three specific phenomena, subtle are long lasting, gross bodies, born form mother and father are perishable.*

Intellect, ego, mind, senses, organs, and the 5 potentials have all been defined. They all work together to create subtle bodies. Gross bodies are physical bodies comprised of flesh and bones generated from sperm from fathers (male) and eggs from mothers (female). Gross beings and objects originate from gross components.

Subtle bodies are relatively persistent since they endure after physical bodies die and can be overcome only through Self-knowledge. Physical bodies, on the other hand, are perishable and fleeting.

पूर्वोत्पन्नमसक्तं नियतं महदादिसूक्ष्मपर्यन्तम् ।
संसरति निरुपभोगं भावैरधिवासितं लिङ्गम् ॥ ४० ॥

pūrva-utpannam asaktaṃ niyatam mahat ādi sūkṣma-paryaṇtam ।
saṃsarati nirupa-bhogaṃ bhāvaiḥ adhivāsitaṃ liṅgam ॥

**– 40 –**

*(subtle bodies are) first born/primeval, unconfined, permanent,*
*composed of intellect with other subtle principles,*
*transmigrates without being able to experience,*
*with components, and merging.*

Subtle bodies are first in the sequence of creation since they are directly born from primordial Nature. Because they are subtle and formless, they are not restricted and can penetrate any physical body. They persist even after the demise of gross bodies. Intellect, ego, mind, senses, and organs comprise subtle bodies. Subtle bodies cannot experience objects without the aid of gross bodies, just as an internet signal cannot work without an electronic device such as a computer or cell phone. As a result, they transmigrate from one gross body to another. There are some other components (qualities) to subtle bodies (which will be discussed in a later passage) that merge in primordial Nature at the time of resolution.

चित्रं यथाऽऽश्रयमृते स्थाण्वादिभ्यो विना यथा छाया ।
तद्वद्विना विशेषैर्न तिष्ठति निराश्रयं लिङ्गम् ॥ ४१ ॥

citraṃ yathā āśrayam ṛte sthāṇvādibhyo vinā yathā chāyā ।
tadvat vinā viśeṣaiḥ na tiṣṭhati nirāśrayaṃ liṅgam ॥

**– 41 –**

*As a painting without a support (wall or canvas)*
*and shadow without an object like stump etc. cannot be.*
*Similarly, subtle bodies cannot function without gross bodies.*

A drawing or painting cannot exist without its support, such as paper, canvas, or wall and a shadow cannot exist without an object, such as a tree stump, etc. to cast the shadow. Similarly, without the assistance of gross bodies, subtle bodies cannot function or experience material Nature. (Although internet signals can be found all around us, they cannot be used without the assistance of an electronic device). Subtle bodies are made up of 13 elements = 1 intellect + 1 ego + 1 mind + 5 senses + 5 organs.

पुरुषार्थहेतुकमिदं निमित्तनैमित्तिकप्रसङ्गेन ।
एते स्मृता विशेषाः शान्ता घोराश्च मूढाश्च ॥ ४२ ॥

puruṣārtha-hetukam idaṃ nimitta naimittika prasaṅgena ।
prakṛteḥ vibhutva yogat naṭavat vyavatiṣṭhate liṅgam ॥

**– 42 –**

*This subtle body is for the sake of enjoyment and liberation,*
*by the attainment of cause (a/dharma) and effect (body) functions,*
*primordial Nature having power of manifold manifestation.*

In a previous section, it is said that subtle bodies function with the assistance of gross bodies, but for what purpose?

Assembly activities, according to passages 17 and 21, are intended for delight and liberation. The subtle body is both an assembly and an effect of the *Primordial Cause*. It is there for the experience and enjoyment of Nature, as well as the realization of the Spirit's freedom.

How? If all subtle bodies exist for the sake of experiencing and Liberation, what is the difference between them, or rather, why do some achieve spiritual freedom while others stay trapped in cycles of worldly suffering? What is the source of these cycles of suffering?

Subtle bodies act in various ways based on their attainment of righteousness, harmony, or order (dharma), unrighteousness, disharmony, or disorder (adharma), and gross (physical) bodies. *Primordial Cause* manifests in multiple bodies for the achievement of varied experiences according to their attainment of dharma and adharma, much like an actor who plays numerous roles in a theatrical play or in movies. (Sometimes an actor plays a king or queen, other times a beggar, and so on.)

सांसिद्धिकाश्च भावाः प्राकृतिका वैकृतिकाश्च धर्माद्याः ।
करणाऽश्रयिणः कार्याऽऽश्रयिणश्च कललाद्याः ॥ ४३ ॥
sāṃsiddhikāḥ ca bhāvāḥ prakṛtikāḥ vaikṛtikāḥ ca dharmādhāḥ ।
dṛṣṭāḥ karaṇāśrayiṇaḥ kāryāśrayiṇaḥ ca kalalādyāḥ ॥

**– 43 –**

*Qualities such as righteousness, etc. can be natural and incidental, the natural are self-existing, and incidental are by association, etc. Natural and incidental qualities are associated with instruments, qualities such as embryo, fetus, etc. are associated with gross bodies.*

In an earlier passage, it is said that subtle bodies attain cycles of suffering (saṃsāra) and liberation from suffering through the dharma, etc. In this passage, those qualities are classified as (1) natural and (2) acquired.

Natural qualities like heat in a fire are self-coexistent. Dharma, wisdom, detachment, and mastery are innate natural qualities in some people, such as Kapila, the founder of Sāṅkhya philosophy. (This means that they were born with certain traits and did not have to work to attain them.)

These traits may also be incidental in some people, such as the different sages, saints, and world teachers we know, who attained them through spiritual practice, worship, and meditation.

Similarly, qualities like unrighteousness, greed, hatred, and violence can be both natural and incidental in some people. These qualities are natural in deranged and evil people, but they can also be caused by interactions or association with malicious people. We can be born with them or develop them, nature, nurture, or a combination of both.

Qualities like dharma, adharma, and so on are related to subtle bodies, which mean they are associated with intellect, ego, and mind.[16]

---

[16] This is similar to modern *'behaviorism'* or *'behavioral neuroscience'*, which investigates the role of nature, nurture, conditioning, and physiology as they pertain to 'qualities' of behavior.

According to passage 39, gross bodies are born from mother and father. What are their characteristics? Gross bodies are associated with qualities such as embryo, fetus, childhood, youth, and old age, among others.

धर्मेण गमनमूर्ध्वं गमनमधस्ताद्भवत्यधर्मेण ।
ज्ञानेन चाऽपवर्गो विपर्ययादिष्यते बन्धः ॥ ४४ ॥

dharmeṇa gamanam ūrdhva gamanam adhastād bhavati adharmeṇa ।
jñānena ca apavargaḥ viparyayāt iṣyate bandhaḥ ॥

**– 44 –**

*By the dharma, it (the subtle body) goes to the higher region,*
*by adharma, it goes to the lower region,*
*by self-knowledge, it attains liberation,*
*and by ignorance, it attains bondage.*

When we perform beneficial actions, such expressions are imprinted in the mind and intellect (subtle body). As the subtle body attains greater sāttva, it attains higher regions, meaning superior bodies. (Saṃsāra is a cycle, which means it has a higher and lower region. The existence of different worlds or realms is likewise allowed here. Thus, through attaining sāttva, the subtle body can reach another realm with superior extraterrestrial bodies or a superior human body).

When we commit harmful acts, such expressions become imprinted in the intellect and mind, and the subtle body gains additional tamās and rājas. When the subtle body has a higher concentration of rājas and tamās, it travels to the lower region or realm where rājas and tamās are more prevalent. Subtle bodies can be born in an inferior life form such as an animal, tree, or plant, or an inferior human birth due to rājas and tamās predomination.

This cycle of attaining a higher or lower region or realm is known as saṃsāra. Tamās will send you to a lower region, and sāttva takes you to a higher region, but neither will give you freedom from it. Even the highest sāttvic expression is vulnerable to suffering because it is part of the cycle of coming and going. So, how do we realize liberation from this cycle?

We can realize liberation through Self-knowledge. Through acquiring a correct understanding of Self and not-Self, manifest and unmanifest Nature, we shall learn that it is only the 'not-Self' (never the 'true-Self') that moves to higher and lower regions to experience pleasure and pain. Nonetheless, we tend to superimpose the not-Self's qualities on the Self. When we differentiate between Self (Spirit/Puruṣa) and not-Self (Nature/Prakṛti), we will never superimpose any qualities on the Self, and therefore we understand the Self as ever-free of any phenomena. By ignorance, we attain bondage by superimposing qualities of not-Self onto the Self.

वैराग्यात्प्रकृतिलयः संसारो भवति राजसाद्रागात् ।
ऐश्वर्यादविघातो विपर्ययात्तद्विपर्यासः ॥ ४५ ॥

vairāgyat prakṛtilayaḥ saṃsāro bhavati rājasāt rāgāt ।
aiśvaryāt avighātaḥ viparyayāt tad viparyāsaḥ ॥

— 45 —

*Absorption in nature is by (mere) dispassion;*
*attainment of the cycle of saṃsāra is by passion,*
*by mastery, there is no impediment, and by the reverse, the contrary.*

We attain absorption in Nature by mere dispassion, which means that when we have only dispassion, but no Self-knowledge, we misidentify the Self as subtle body (intellect-ego-mind) and perceive oneness with them. We achieve absorption in Nature through this type of mental veneration (meditation). This suggests that we experience a type of temporary release from affliction, but not complete liberation. We engage in worldly activities due to our passion (lack of dispassion) and undergo the saṃsāra cycle of pleasure and pain.

We can develop many seemingly extraordinary skills and abilities through long-term meditation on the intellect and its qualities. As a result, we become capable of accomplishing things that other untrained individuals find difficult.

Moreover, in the absence of these skills and abilities, we remain unable to perceive the desired object or goal, meaning that we can only imagine or fantasize about things that we are unable to actualize.

एष प्रत्ययसर्गो विपर्ययाऽशक्तितुष्टिसिद्ध्याख्यः ।
गुणवैषम्यविमर्दात् तस्य च भेदास्तु पञ्चाशत् ॥ ४६ ॥

eṣah pratyayasargaḥ viparyaya-aśakti tuṣṭiḥ siddhi-ākhyaḥ ।
guṇa-vaiṣamya-vimardāt tasya ca bhedāḥ tu pāñcāśat ॥

**– 46 –**

*This creation of intellect, termed as abstraction/misapprehension, disability, contentment, and attainment.*
*By disparity of influence of qualities,*
*subdivisions are 50 in number.*

Dharma, adharma, wisdom, ignorance, and so on, these are all qualities of the intellect. As a result, this intellectual creation has four components: (1) *abstraction*, (2) *disability*, (3) *contentment*, and (4) *attainment*.

1. ***Abstraction* = ignorance**. It is also explained as the 5-fold afflictions in the *Yoga Sutras* of Patañjali, (अविद्याऽस्मितारागद्वेष-अभिनिवेशाः ignorance, pride, attachment, aversion, and fear).

2. ***Disability* = the defect** that prevents us from understanding things as they are.

3. ***Contentment* = satisfaction** through attainment of dharma, dispassion, etc.

4. ***Attainment* = Self-knowledge** through the discernment of Spirit and Nature, and some other supernatural qualities.

There are 50 subdivisions of these 4-fold qualities, based on the fluctuations of the three qualities (3-guṇas).

पञ्च विपर्ययभेदा भवन्त्यशक्तिस्तु करणवैकल्यात् ।
अष्टाविंशतिभेदा तुष्टिर्नवधाऽष्टधा सिद्धिः ॥ ४७ ॥

pañca viparyaya bhedāḥ bhavaṁti aśaktiḥ ca karaṇa vaikalyāt ।
aṣṭāvimśāti bhedāḥ tuṣṭiḥ navadhā aṣṭadhā siddhiḥ ॥

**– 47 –**

*Abstraction is 5-fold,*
*the defect of instrumental disability is 28-fold,*
*contentment is 9-fold,*
*and attainment is 8-fold.*

The fluctuation of three qualities, – sāttva, rājas, and tamās – results in a 5-fold ***abstraction*** (misperception; misapprehension; conceptual error):

1. **Ignorance** = no clear discernment of Self and not-Self
2. **Pride** = identifying with the not-Self rather than the Self
3. **Attachment** = seeking fulfillment through materialism
4. **Aversion** = desire for fulfillment is restricted by something
5. **Fear** = of losing objects of attachment / fear of death

***Disability*** is 28-fold due to the various defects in instruments and intellect, which will be explained later. ***Contentment*** is 9-fold, and ***attainment*** is 8-fold.

भेदस्तमसोऽष्टविधो मोहस्य च दशविधो महामोहः ।
तामिस्रोऽष्टदशधा तथा भवत्यन्धतामिस्रः ॥ ४८ ॥

bhedaḥ tamasaḥ aṣṭa vidhaḥ mohasaya ca daśavidhaḥ maha-mohaḥ ।
tāmisraḥ aṣṭādaśadhā tathā bhavati aṅdhatā misraḥ ॥

**– 48 –**

*Ignorance is 8-fold, illusion (pride) is also 8-fold,*
*extreme illusion (attachment) is 10-fold,*
*darkness (aversion) and utter darkness (fear) are of 18 fold.*

Ignorance is the result of misidentification with Nature, which is 8-fold: (1) intellect, (2) ego, (3) mind, with (+5) five potentials. These eight abilities appear or feel like the Self, however, this is an illusion, which means that they are not the Self. 'Illusion' means 'not as it appears'. All of these aspects of personality appear to make up the Self, however, this is an illusion. These are simply instruments of experiencing but not the Self. Taking these eight elements as Self is a source of pride. These eight provide a way of interacting with the objects of Awareness. We take pride in our ability to process what we experience. This sort of pride is misplaced.

Sound, touch, form, taste, and smell appear as 5 worldly (gross) and 5 otherworldly (subtle) variations, resulting in a 10-fold extreme illusion. The 'extreme illusion' is the grand collective 'object of Awareness', everything that is experienced or experienceable – the universe and everything in it, all matter (gross) and energy (subtle).

The variety of 10-fold worldly and otherworldly (gross and subtle) objects of Awareness + the 8-fold ability to experience those objects is what is meant by *"18-fold darkness"* (aversion) and *"utter darkness"* (fear). (The 8-fold abilities are well listed in the *Yoga Sutras*).

एकादशेन्द्रियवधाः सह बुद्धिवधैरशक्तिरुद्दिष्टा ।
सप्तदशवधा बुद्धेर्विपर्ययात्तुष्टिसिद्धीनाम् ॥ ४९ ॥

ekādaśa iṅdriyavadhāḥ saha buddhi vadhaiḥ aśaktiḥ uddiṣṭā ।
saptadaśa vadhāḥ buddheḥ viparyayāt tuṣṭi siddhīnām ॥

**– 49 –**

*Disability is 28-fold; there are 11 defects in 11 instruments,*
*(5 senses, 5 organs, + 1 intellect),*
*17 defects are associated with the intellect*
*by the division of ignorance, contentment, and attainment.*

There are 28 disabilities, according to passage 47. Eleven defects are associated with 11 instruments: 5 senses, 5 organs, and 1 intellect. We can be disabled in one or more senses, such as being blind or deaf, for example. We can also have a disability affecting our physical organs of action, such as paralysis. We can be disabled due to a variety of mental conditions. This is what *"11 defects in 11 instruments"* means.

Disabilities associated with intellect are 17 by the division of *contentment* and *attainment*. There are 9 defects associated with *contentment* and 8 defects associated with *attainment*.

आध्यात्मिक्यश्चतस्रः प्रकृत्युपादानकालभाग्याख्याः ।
बाह्या विषयोपरमात्पञ्च नव तुष्टयोऽभिमताः ॥ ५० ॥

ādhyātmikāḥ catasraḥ prakṛti upādāna kāla bhāgya ākhyāḥ ।
bāhyāḥ viṣaya uparamāt pañca nava tuṣṭayaḥ abhimatāḥ ॥

– 50 –

*Inner are 4-fold, relating to Nature, means, time and luck,*
*outer are 5-fold due to dispassion from 5-fold sense objects,*
*thus contentment is 9-fold.*

According to passage 47, contentment is 9-fold, internal is 4-fold, and external is 5-fold.

### *4-Fold Inner (Ideological) Contentments*

1. ***Science***: Inner contentment is a 4-fold relationship (science, pretense, time, and luck). The first is when someone understands primordial Nature and its effects but fails to understand the Spirit, yet remains satisfied with a mere understanding of Nature. Most societies use science to try to comprehend Nature and its effects, and they are satisfied with their findings. This is referred to as 'natural' contentment. They may find some degree of satisfaction, but they will

never be liberated from suffering since ultimate freedom from suffering is only available through Self-knowledge.

2. ***Outer Renunciation***: The second is when someone, without realizing the distinction between Nature and Spirit, and the true nature of the Self, adopts the outer symbols of renunciation, such as wearing monk's robes, and pretends to be Self-realized by donning all the symbolic attire. Although one may experience some satisfaction, such a person does not experience liberation because they lack Self-knowledge.

3. ***Time***: The third is when someone does not make an effort to understand the true nature of the Self, by distinguishing between Spirit and primal Nature, and instead believes that liberation is going to occur in time. They believe that time is the cause of liberation and that, when the moment is right, they will be liberated. These types of thinkers may feel some satisfaction from their beliefs, but they do not realize liberation because it is only possible through Self-knowledge.

4. ***Luck***: The fourth is when some people assume that liberation occurs by luck. If it is a person's fate to attain liberation, they will do so without any effort. These individuals are also not liberated.

### *5-Fold Outer (Circumstantial) Contentments*

5. — 9.: ***Withdrawal***: Outer contentment is 5-fold due to dispassion from five sense objects such as (5) ***sound***, (6) ***touch***, (7) ***form***, (8) ***smell***, and (9) ***taste***. These are the qualities of objects of pleasure that appeal to and delight the senses. Pain and pleasure are two sides of the same coin. When someone pursues pleasure, they also experience suffering and frustration. On the other hand, when someone abandons the pursuit of sense objects as a means to achieve happiness, identity, or satisfaction (materialism), they break the cycle of pleasure and pain and thereby achieve outer contentment. This is called 'withdrawal'.

For example, money is a method to obtain desirable pleasure objects and to earn that kind of money; a person must perform numerous difficult tasks. Some are forced to work for awful bosses. People will sometimes commit criminal offenses to earn enormous sums of money. As a result, there is a great deal of suffering and frustration in the chase of money, as well as frustration in defending that money, because when someone has a lot of money, other people crave it, resulting in fear of thieves, the government, and other adversaries. Furthermore, when the balance becomes depleted by spending it on sense objects, there is pain and dissatisfaction.

When we become addicted to seeking pleasure by purchasing material objects to satisfy a desire for happiness, it can harm both our physical and mental health. Worse, when we lose our financial prosperity for any reason, we experience even greater pain and frustration. Thus, there is pain and frustration involved with the pursuit of money for sense pleasures, there is pain and frustration associated with its protection, and there is pain and frustration associated with its loss.

Whoever understands all of these faults associated with sense objects achieves dispassion toward chasing happiness, fulfillment, and identity through materialistic wealth, and achieves 5-fold contentment. We may *'withdraw'* from these cycles, from society, or the pursuit of materialism and obtain relative contentment, but this is not freedom from suffering since only Self-knowledge leads to liberation.

ऊहः शब्दोऽध्ययनं दुःखविघातास्त्रयः सुहृत्प्राप्तिः ।
दानं च सिद्धयोऽष्टौ सिद्धेः पूर्वोऽङ्कुशस्त्रिविधः ॥ ५१ ॥

ūhaḥ śabdaḥ adhyayanaṃ duhkha-vighātāḥ trayaḥ sukṛt prāptiḥ ।
dānaṃ ca siddhayaḥ aṣṭau siddheḥ pūrvaḥ aṅkuśaḥ trividhaḥ ॥

– 51 –

*Reasoning, listening, study, prevention of the 3-fold suffering,*
*attainment of good company, and purity are 8-fold attainment,*
*there are 3-fold obstructions for these attainments.*
*(5-fold abstractions, 28-fold disability, and 9-fold contentment)*

What exactly is reality? What exactly is absolute Truth? What exactly is liberation? Furthermore, how can we realize Truth and liberation? Someone who is striving to find answers to these questions and understands the true nature of the Self recognizes the difference between Nature and Spirit and therefore realizes liberation.

### *8-Fold Attainment*

1. ***Reasoning***: The first attainment is reasoning, which is required to reach conclusions. Someone who lacks the capacity of proper reasoning will be unable to distinguish between cause and effect, as well as Nature and Spirit.

2. ***Listening***: The second attainment is to understand meanings by listening to teachers and teachings.

3. **Study**: The third attainment is the study of spiritual teachings.

4. 5. 6. ***Prevention of 3-fold suffering***: The fourth, fifth, and sixth attainments are (4) the prevention of personal (inner) suffering, (5) circumstantial (outer) suffering, and (6) natural (extraordinary) suffering. When a person realizes that the Spirit is free of Nature and its effects, they know that various types of suffering are associated with Nature, not the Spirit.

7. ***Good Company***: The seventh attainment is the company of a realized instructor, earnest classmates, and supportive friends; we can come to a proper understanding of Spirit and Nature through discussions with teachers, classmates, friends, and other forms of 'good company'.

8. ***Purity***: The eighth accomplishment is purity, which includes being free from inner and outer conflicts, doubts, misapprehension, and self-ignorance.

Thus, attainments are 8-fold, (1) reasoning, (2) listening, (3) study, (4,5,6) prevention of 3-fold suffering, (7) good company and (8) purity. As previously mentioned, these attainments are impeded by three obstructions: *abstraction*, *disability*, and *contentment*. Under the influence of these obstructions whoever fails to recognize the distinction between the Self (Spirit/Puruṣa) and the not-Self (Nature/Prakṛti) remains trapped in the cycle of suffering (saṃsāra).

न विना भावैर्लिङ्गं न विना लिङ्गैर्न भावनिर्वृत्तिः ।
लिङ्गाख्यो भावाख्यस्तस्माद् द्विविधः प्रवर्तते सर्गः ॥ ५२ ॥

na vinā bhāvaiḥ liṅgaṃ na vinā liṅgena bhāva nirvṛttiḥ ।
liṅgena bhāvākhyaḥ tasmāt dvedhā pravartate sargaḥ ॥

– 52 –

*Without the creation of disposition,*
*there cannot be creation of symbols,*
*without the creation of symbols there cannot be dispositions,*
*therefore, there is a 2-fold creation, symbolic and dispositional.*

As pointed out in passages 44 and 45, abstraction, disability, contentment, as well as attainment from passage 46 are dispositional creations, which mean that these are qualities that belong to the intellect – they are *subjective*.

Symbolic creation is the creation of elements, subtle and gross bodies, sense objects, and so on - they are *objective*.

**Q**: Why are there two types of creation?

**A**: Because one sort of creation cannot exist without the other. It's similar to the chicken and egg problem. They both rely on one another for existence. Symbolic creation cannot occur without dispositional creation. We cannot obtain a subtle or physical body without dharma, adharma, misapprehension, and self-ignorance. We cannot attain/commit dharma, adharma, or have Self-ignorance unless we have a subtle and physical body.

Subject-object relativity, both dispositional and symbolic, is a timeless cycle in which we cannot determine which came first. Both creations will disappear if the cycle is stopped by the correct understanding of Nature and Spirit - Self and not-Self.

अष्टविकल्पो दैवस्तैर्यग्योनश्च पञ्चधा भवति ।
मानुष्यश्चैकविधः समासतो भौतिकः सर्गः ॥ ५३ ॥

aṣṭa vikalpaḥ daivaḥ tairyagyonaḥ ca pañcadhā bhavati ।
mānuṣakaḥ ca eka vidhaḥ samasataḥ bhautikaḥ sargaḥ ॥

**– 53 –**

*Divine bodies are 8-fold,*
*lower life is 5-fold, the human body is single-fold,*
*and thus the world of living beings is briefly explained.*

It is thought that there are numerous worlds and dimensions, and that the beings who inhabit those worlds/dimensions differ. 14 separate worlds/dimensions are provided as a model in Indian spiritual traditions.

There are six higher dimensions and seven lower dimensions, with Earth in the middle.

Each realm or dimension has an ideal being or exemplar associated with it. Today, we recognize the 14-world/dimension paradigm as merely a conceptual model used for understanding the plurality of worlds and dimensions. According to classical physics, humans can perceive four dimensions of space-time: length, width, height, and time. So far, the most advanced mathematical equations have been useful in identifying eleven dimensions. So far, we have been unable to validate or refute this type of outlook.

Lower life was considered 5-fold in former times: (1) animals, (2) birds and insects, (3) reptiles, (4) fish, and (5) plants.

Humans are of a single type, which implies they are distinct; they do not fall into the categories of divine beings or inferior life forms.

Reflecting on these serves to explain briefly the vast multiplicity of bodies and worlds, as well as, according to contemporary physics, multiple universes (the multi-verse).

ऊर्ध्वं सत्त्वविशालस्तमोविशालश्च मूलतः सर्गः ।
मध्ये रजोविशालो ब्रह्मादिः स्तम्बपर्यन्तः ॥ ५४ ॥

ūrdhvaṃ sattva-viśālaḥ tamo-viśālaḥ ca mūlataḥ sargaḥ ।
madhye rajo-viśālaḥ brahmādi stamba-prayaṅtaḥ ॥

**– 54 –**

*Sāttva quality is predominant in higher bodies.*
*In lower bodies tamās is predominant, in middle rājas is predominant.*
*Thus, the qualities of bodies from the Creator to plants are explained.*

Everything is built from three qualities: sāttva, rājas, and tamās. The sāttva quality predominates in higher bodies such as even the Creator. As a result, those beings are superior, with a deeper understanding of things, as well as greater intellectual capacity and joy.

Tamās is predominant in lower bodies such as animals, birds, insects, fish, and plants. As a result, those beings have diminished intellectual capacity, dullness, and ignorance.

Because rājas is prominent in humans, there are more activities, greed, competitiveness, ambition, frustration, and so on. Humans aren't as dull as animals and other lower lifeforms, but they're also not as good and pure as higher beings.

These three qualities are always present in all lifeforms, but the amount in which they are distributed differentiates individuals. When there is more sāttva, there is more purity, intelligence, understanding, and so on. There is dullness and darkness when tamās is greater.

तत्र जरामरणकृतं दुःखं प्राप्नोति चेतनः पुरुषः ।
लिङ्गस्याऽविनिवृत्तेस्तस्माद् दुःखं स्वभावेन ॥ ५५ ॥

tatra jarāmaraṇa kṛtaṃ duḥkhaṃ prāpnoti cetanaḥ puruṣaḥ ।
liṅgasya avinivṛtteḥ tasmāt duḥkhaṃ svabhāvena ॥

– 55 –

*Sentient being (Spirit) experiences the pain*
*arising from decay and death there,*
*until the cessation of subtle body, pain is natural.*

All gross bodies, whether higher, middle, or lower, are subject to change, decay, and death. Everything that is composed must eventually decompose. All lifeforms experience pain and suffering as a result of the physical body's birth, decay, and death. Suffering is felt by sentient being (Spirit) as a result of this association with the subtle body. As a result, suffering is inevitable for so long as the relationship with the subtle body persists.

इत्येष प्रकृतिकृतो महदादिविशेषभूतपर्यन्तः ।
प्रतिपुरुषविमोक्षार्थं स्वार्थ इव परार्थ आरम्भः ॥ ५६ ॥
ityeṣaḥ prakṛti kṛtaḥ mahadādi viśeṣa bhūta paryantaḥ ।
prati puruṣa vimokṣārthaṃ svārthe iva pararthe ārambhaḥ ॥

– 56 –

*Thus (from) this creation of intellect to elements of primordial Nature,*
*(Nature; 'all-this') is there for the deliverance of each Spirit,*
*it is done for others' sake as though for its own.*

Thus, primordial Nature and its evolution from intellect, ego, and mind to the elements, different worlds, and bodies are explained. According to passage 21, this association exists for the Spirits' Liberation and the experience of Nature. Primordial Nature manifests itself in various forms for the Liberation of Spirits. Nature gives the Spirit a variety of experiences, and in the end, it delivers Liberation to the Spirit by the proper understanding of the Self and not-Self. Nature accomplishes everything for the sake of Spirit, not for the sake of itself.

वत्सविवृद्धिनिमित्तं क्षीरस्य यथा प्रवृत्तिरज्ञस्य ।
पुरुषविमोक्षनिमित्तं तथा प्रवृत्तिः प्रधानस्य ॥ ५७ ॥

vatsa vivṛddhi nimittaṃ kṣīrasya yathā pravṛttiḥ ajñasya ।
puruṣa vimokṣa nimittaṃ tathā pravṛttiḥ pradhānasya ॥

**– 57 –**

*As it is the function of inert milk (an unintelligent substance)*
*to nourish the calf,*
*similarly, Nature functions for the Liberation of Spirit.*

**Objection**: If Nature is inert and Spirit is sentient, how can inert Nature have intellectual activity in and of itself?

**Response**: This question is invalid because it has been established that even insentient entities can engage in intelligent actions.

For example, milk that is inert and made from grass and water consumed by a cow is activated by the birth of a calf for its nourishment, and it is deactivated by itself once the calf is well nourished.

There is a deep and indisputable beauty in how matter, energy, and forces interact in the universe, demonstrating such intelligence that humans can only dimly perceive it, yet matter and energy are inert in that they are insentient.

As such, Nature functions for the Liberation of the Spirit.

औत्सुक्यनिवृत्त्यर्थं यथा क्रियासु प्रवर्तते लोकः ।
पुरुषस्य विमोक्षार्थं प्रवर्त्तते तद्वदव्यक्तम् ॥ ५८ ॥

autsukya nivṛtti-arthaṃ yathā kriyasu pravartate lokaḥ ।
puruṣasya vimokṣārthaṃ pravartate tadvat avyaktam ॥

**– 58 –**

*As people become engaged in various activities*
*for the removal of curiosity and desires,*
*similarly, nature manifest itself for the Liberation of Spirit.*

It has been observed that when people become inquisitive about something or have specific desires, they engage in many different activities to satisfy their curiosity and desires. They experience relief when their curiosity or desire is gratified. Thus, fundamental Nature shows itself as intellect, ego, mind, and so on, offering experiences and Liberation to the Spirit, and then Nature deactivates once its job is done.

रङ्गस्य दर्शयित्वा निवर्तते नर्तकी यथा नृत्यात् ।
पुरुषस्य तथाऽऽत्मानं प्रकाश्य निवर्तते प्रकृतिः ॥ ५९ ॥

raṅgasya darśayitvā nivartate nartakī yathā nṛtyāt ।
puruṣasya tathā ātmānaṃ prakāśya vinivartate prakṛtiḥ ॥

**– 59 –**

*As a dancer returns from her dance performance*
*after presenting her performance to the audience/spectator,*
*similarly, Nature having revealed itself to the Spirit*
*returns and is deactivated.*

As a dancer in full makeup approaches the stage to entertain the audience and perform her dance, and when her performance is complete and she has satisfied her audience, she returns home. Similarly, Nature manifests itself in many forms to provide the Spirit with experience and liberation, and then it returns.

### *Points for Reflection*

- Passage 39: **Existence of Gross and Subtle Bodies**. Today, we might think of 'gross' and 'subtle' bodies in terms of a physical body (gross) and an energetic or psychological body (subtle), which can also be thought of as 'mind' in a general sense, or 'soul' in an individual sense.
- Passage 44: **'Liberating knowledge' is from knowledge (jñāna) brought about by discernment and not dispassion (vairāgya)**. Dispassion is a result of clear discernment, the differentiation, and understanding of Nature and Spirit. Intellectual understanding or discernment matures first into firm intellectual conviction and from there to a deep experiential revelation of the Truth of Self. This breakthrough is called 'Realization'.
- Passage 44: **bondage is from ignorance (lack of knowledge)**. The intellect-ego-mind (3-fold mind/inner-instrument) either doesn't know the Truth, or understands incorrectly. Both ignorance and error imply a lack of knowledge. As a result, we FEEL trapped and bound, due to either not knowing the true-Self, or clinging to the false identity in which we tend to identify with the body-mind organism, or with the subtle-body as self. Sāṅkhya's special form of inquiry + reflective meditation removes the ignorance and error.
- Passage 45: **Dispassion, sometimes called 'detachment', without Self-knowledge, is a form of rejection or escapism** and therefore not true dispassion. Meditative absorption must be based on the foundation of liberating knowledge.
- Passages 23, 45, 65 are the only passages that allude to 'yogic' practices. Yoga as a practice is a system of mastery aimed at purity, meaning a sāttvic and dharmic life, that leads to true discernment and dispassion, which ultimately leads to Realization and Liberation. Chapter 8, passage 45 explains the error of false dispassion as meditation practiced without the necessary liberating knowledge.

# 9
# Knowledge & Freedom

नानाविधैरुपायैरुपकारिण्यनुपकारिणः पुंसः ।
गुणवत्यगुणस्य सतस्तस्याऽर्थमपार्थकं चरति ॥ ६० ॥

nanavidhaiḥ upāyaiḥ upakāriṇi anupakāriṇaḥ puṃsaḥ ।
guṇavati aguṇasya sataḥ tasya artham apārthakaṃ carati ॥

– 60 –

*Nature, with all its qualities, functions with various means for the Spirit that has no qualities and is neutral/unreactive without expecting any result for its own.*

To express itself in front of the Spirit, Nature displays itself through various bodies (celestial, human, animal, etc.), qualities (sāttva, rājas, and tamās), and sense-objects (sound, touch, form, etc.). When the difference between Spirit and Nature is understood, it returns or is deactivated once its purpose has been fulfilled.

As some people enjoy selflessly serving others or society without expecting anything in return, a reactive Nature serves an unreactive Spirit without expecting anything in return. *"Nature manifests itself in various ways and presents experiences to the Spirit and returns after it has presented Liberation to the Spirit, without any expectation"*, reveals that experiences and Liberation are presented for the sake of Spirit, not Nature.

प्रकृतेः सुकुमारतरं न किञ्चिदस्तीति मे मतिर्भवति ।
या दृष्टाऽस्मीति पुनर्न दर्शनमुपैति पुरुषस्य ॥ ६१ ॥

prakṛteḥ sukumārataraṃ na kiñcit asti iti me matiḥ bhavati ।
yā dṛṣṭā asmi iti punaḥ na darśanam upaiti puruṣasya ॥

– 61 –

*Nothing, in my opinion, is more sensitive than Nature;*
*once aware of having been seen/understood (by Spirit),*
*Nature does not again expose itself to the gaze of Spirit.*

**Doubt**: Is it possible for Nature to reappear after liberation and restart the saṃsāra cycle of suffering to re-bind the Spirit once again?

**Response**: No, it is not possible since, once known, Truth, like any other object in the universe, cannot be unknown.

Iśvarakṛṣṇa, the author, expresses his perspective on Nature by comparing it to a traditional woman from ancient times. Because a traditional woman dislikes being seen by other men, if she believes she has exposed herself to the sight of other men in any condition, she will return and hide herself from the sight of other men.

Nature is exceedingly sensitive; once fully understood by Spirit, it will never appear again, once known, it cannot be unknown. The Truth of Nature, once seen beyond its illusory appearance, cannot be unseen.

तस्मान्न बध्यतेऽध्दा न मुच्यते नापि संसरति कश्चित् ।
संसरति बध्यते मुच्यते च नानाऽऽश्रया प्रकृतिः ॥ ६२ ॥

tasmāt na badhyate-asau na mucyate na api saṃsarati kaścit ।
saṃsarati badhyate mucyate ca nānāśrayā prakṛtiḥ ॥

– 62 –

*Truly, not any Spirit is bound, nor is released, nor migrates;*
*but nature alone, in relation to various beings,*
*is bound, is released, and migrates.*

Because Nature is reactive and has qualities, all action potential and changes belong to Nature rather than the Spirit, which is unreactive and devoid of qualities. Spirit is eternally free of all natural modifications and functions. It is witness-Consciousness. It is not bound, it is not released (liberated), and it does not migrate in the saṃsāra cycle of suffering. All of these qualities belong to Nature, not to the Spirit (albeit they are superimposed on the Spirit in the same way as the qualities of fire are superimposed on a heated metal rod).

रूपैः सप्तभिरेव तु बध्नात्यात्मानमात्मना प्रकृतिः ।
सैव च पुरषार्थं प्रति विमोचयत्येकरूपेण ॥ ६३ ॥

rūpaiḥ saptabhiḥ eva tu badhnāti ātmānam ātmanā prakṛtiḥ ।
saiva ca purṣārthaṃ prati vimocayati eka rūpeṇa ॥

**– 63 –**

*Nature binds itself by seven modes;*
*later nature releases itself from self-created bondage*
*by one mode/quality for the Liberation of spirit.*

Nature, it is said in an earlier passage, binds and frees itself from bondage. How?

Nature binds itself with its seven qualities – dharma and adharma, passion and dispassion, mastery and lack of mastery, and ignorance – just as a caterpillar binds itself into a cocoon and then frees itself from that same cocoon after reaching maturity, as explained earlier in passages 43, 44, and 45.

Then, by one quality, – Self-knowledge – Nature releases itself from its self-created bondage.

एवं तत्वाऽभ्यासान्नाऽस्मि न मे नाऽहमित्यपरिशेषम् ।
अविपर्ययाद्विशुद्धं केवलमुत्पद्यते ज्ञानम् ॥ ६४ ॥

evaṃ tattvābhyāsāt na asmi na me na aham iti apariśeṣam ।
aviparyayāt viśuddhaṃ kevalam utpadyate jñānam ॥

**– 64 –**

*Thus by the analysis of real and unreal (Spirit and Nature)*
*pure knowledge is born that is free of any doubts and projection,*
*that is – I am not this ( body mind sense complex),*
*it is not mine ( body mind senses etc.), nor am I ego.*

In the preceding passage, it is explicitly stated that Self-knowledge leads to freedom. How is that Self-knowledge attained?

The analysis of Self and not-Self leads to self-knowledge. True-Self is the Spirit that is free of all qualities and modifications, and the not-Self is Nature with its effects and qualities. All the changes, modifications, and activities belong to Nature and not to the Self. Such ultimate, pure, and doubt-free understanding leads to realizing freedom, which is – *"I am not the body-mind organism", "The qualities and activities of the body-mind's senses do not belong to me", "I, the Spirit, am different than the egoic sense of 'I'"*. Body-mind, ego-sense, and so forth, with their qualities and actions, are all fluctuations of Nature, and hence they are all not-Self. Spirit, witness-Consciousness, is the Self that remains unaffected by Nature and its effects.

तेन निवृत्तप्रसवामर्थवशात् सप्तरूपविनिवृत्ताम् ।
प्रकृतिं पश्यति पुरुषः प्रेक्षकवदवस्थितः स्वस्थः ॥ ६५ ॥

tena nivṛttapraśavā arthavaśāt sapta rūpa vinivṛttām ।
prakṛtiṃ paśyati puruṣaḥ prekṣakavat avasthitaḥ svacchaḥ ॥

**– 65 –**

*Nature has ceased its creation (of afflictions)*
*by the cessation of 7-fold binding qualities,*
*thus by Self-knowledge,*
*Self-realized Spirit witnesses Nature as a spectator.*

What comes after Self-realization? Spirit, having recognized its true immortal, unchanging nature via Self-knowledge, sees Nature – which has ceased from causing affliction through the cessation of 7-fold binding attributes – similar to how a spectator witnesses a dancer's performance without being affected by it. (In a modern sense, we might say that it is similar to watching a movie with all its action, drama, passion, and so forth, but once the movie is over and we leave the cinema and go back to daily life, we remain unaffected by the movie in the sense that the movie is an appearance rather than the reality.)

दृष्टा मयेत्युपेक्षक एको दृष्टाऽहमित्युपरमत्यन्या ।
सति संयोगेऽपि तयोः प्रयोजनं नास्ति सर्गस्य ॥ ६६ ॥

dṛṣṭā mayā iti upekṣakaḥ ekaḥ dṛṣṭā aham iti uparamati anya ।
sati saṃyoge-api prayojanaṃ nāsti sargasya ॥

**– 66 –**

*Spirit desists, because it has seen (realized) Nature;*
*Nature does so, because it has been seen.*
*In their union, there is no motive for creation.*

In an earlier passage, it was said that Spirit and Nature need each other for experience and Liberation, much as a blind and a lame person work together for the same. Spirit sees Nature as it truly is through the analysis of the real and unreal, and as a result, it starts dissociating itself from Nature and its effects. Nature also desists because it is fully understood as it is.

**Doubt**: Nature and Spirit are eternal and omnipresent, their union continues forever. Why would creation come to an end?

**Response**: It will come to an end because there is no purpose for creation after the realization of Nature and Spirit; their union is not the cause of creation. Rather, the motive of experience and Liberation is the cause of creation. Moreover, once that motivation has been fulfilled, there is no need for future creation. Like the relationship between a loan giver and a loan taker, after the loan is repaid, there is no reason for these two people to interact with each other.

सम्यग्ज्ञानाधिगमाद् धर्मादीनामकारणप्राप्तौ ।
तिष्ठति संस्कारवशाच्चक्रभ्रमिवद् धृतशरीरः ॥ ६७ ॥

samyak-jñāna adhigamāt dharmadīnām akāraṇa prāptau ।
tiṣṭhati saṃskāra vaśāt cakra bhramivat dhṛta śarīraḥ ॥

**– 67 –**

*By attainment of perfect knowledge,*
*virtue and the rest become causeless,*
*yet Spirit remains a while invested with body,*
*as the potter's wheel continues whirling from the effect of momentum.*

Spirit no longer identifies with the not-Self, Nature, and its effects after attaining perfect knowledge (complete understanding of Spirit and Nature, untainted by doubts or false projections). Influencing aspects of Nature, such as dharma, adharma, and so forth, lose their causal influence to bind the Spirit (perhaps because the Spirit can never actually be bound; it only feels bound). However, the Spirit stays temporarily invested with the body due to the effect of momentum, similar to how a potter's wheel continues to spin after the pot has been formed. It is analogous to unplugging a spinning electric fan in a more modern meaning. Although no more power is being supplied to the spinning blades, they continue to turn for a short time as the momentum dissipates.

Whoever attains Self-knowledge and is fully Self-realized does not die of realization. They remain in bodily form for a time, never again afflicted by the three sorts of suffering.

In the study of spiritual philosophy, two sorts of liberation are explained: (1) release from suffering while living (jīvanmukti) and (2) liberation after death (videhamukti). Whoever has attained self-knowledge is free of suffering while living, and after death, the physical body does not reincarnate to continue the saṃsāra cycle of suffering. Like a potter's wheel or the fan analogy above, all who have realized the Self do not suddenly die and shed the body, but stay in physical form until the end of the physical body. Dharma, adharma, and so on become like roasted seeds that remain but cannot germinate into sprouts.

प्राप्ते शरीरभेदे चरितार्थत्वात् प्रधानविनिवृत्तौ ।
ऐकान्तिकमात्यन्तिकमुभयं कैवल्यमाप्नोति ॥ ६८ ॥

prāpte śarīrabhede caritārthatvāt pradhāna vinivṛtteḥ ।
aikāṅtikam ātyaṅtikam ubhayaṃ kaivalyaṃ prāpnoti ॥

**– 68 –**

*Having fulfilled its purpose,*
*Nature ceases to function completely after the end of the physical body*
*thus Spirit attains Liberation that is absolute and eternal.*

What kind of liberation is realized?

Nature serves to provide the Spirit with experience and Liberation. Nature, having served its purpose, ceases to function completely after the death of the physical body, granting us absolute and eternal Liberation; absolute because the limiting obstacle of the physical body no longer remains, and eternal because there will be no rebirth in the saṃsāra cycle of suffering.

पुरुषार्थज्ञानमिदं गुह्यं परमर्षिणा समाख्यातम् ।
स्थित्युत्पत्तिप्रलयाश्चिन्त्यन्ते यत्र भूतानाम् ॥ ६९ ॥

puruṣārtha jñānam idaṃ guhyaṃ paramarṣiṇā samākhyātam ।
sthiti utpatti pralayaḥ cintyaṅte yatṛa bhūtānām ॥

– 69 –

*This sacred and profound wisdom is shared by great sage Kapila*
*that leads to liberation*
*where origin, existence, and end of creation are explained.*

Great sage Kapila, out of compassion for others, presents this knowledge of Self and not-Self, introducing 25 principles, the understanding of which leads to freedom from 3-fold suffering, which is difficult to overcome otherwise. This wisdom is *profound* because it is beyond the reach of ordinary minds, *sacred* because it serves in the alleviation of all types of suffering, and hence the greatest of all known types of knowledge. The origin, persistence, and end of creation are discussed in this model of Sāṅkhya philosophy so that we can understand the distinction between Self and not-Self.

***Points for Reflection***

- Passage 61: **Realization** ('seeing Nature for what it is') we think Nature is the reality.
- Passage 64: **Sāṅkhya's key mantra is presented – *"I am not the body-mind. They are not mine. I am Spirit."*** Reflective meditation on this mantra reinforces this liberating knowledge. Pure doubt-free understanding and clear discernment (viveka) leads to freedom, Self-realization, the Realization of the Truth of the mantra. *"I am not the body-mind"* = Sāṅkhya's base teaching
- Passage 64: **Sāṅkhya's key meditative practice (tattvābhyāsa / jñānabhyāsa) is implied**. Once we arrive at a clear doubt-free understanding of Spirit (Puruṣa/true-Self) and Nature (Prakṛti/not-Self), we concentrate on that Truth, on that knowledge, at first with effort until it is effortless. This can be in the form of a gentle and natural contemplation, or as a disciplined practice. In either case, the knowledge or understanding leads to a breakthrough in realizing the Truth of Self, and freedom of binding ignorance and error.

- Passages 23, 45, 65 are the only passages that allude to 'yogic' practices. Chapter 9, passage 63 teaches that virtue and vice,[17] passion and dispassion, mastery and lack thereof, and ignorance are binding factors. Liberation means transcending or being free from their binding influence. Passage 65 explains that after Realization, we are free from Nature's dualistic binding factors, and that all of Nature is revealed to be just a passing show.

- Passage 66: **It can be helpful to think of *"Nature's creation"* or *"creating"* in terms of *"becoming"*.** Nature is always *"becoming"* something new due to its perpetual changing nature. In service to Spirit (the Self), there seems to be a process of *"becoming"* more sāttvic, more dharmic. However, at the point of Self-realization, there is no more *becoming*. Nature has played a role in leading to the realization that there is nothing more to become, nothing more to do. The true-Self is realized to be pure-Spirit, to have always been so and ever will be. Nature (Prakṛti/not-Self) is dynamic *"becoming"* – Spirit (Puruṣa/true-Self) is pure *"being"*.

- After Realization there is Nothing more to *become*, nothing more to improve, nothing more to strive for, nothing more to become or do,[18] because happiness, fulfillment, and identity is clearly known to be the very nature of the true-Self. Nature is seen as a marvelous appearance, an instrument that leads to Realization of the Truth, and Liberation from the false.

---

[17] Sāṅkhya does not teach a doctrine of good and evil. It addresses virtue and vice, the definition of which is 'beneficial to self and others' or 'not beneficial to anyone'. It implies 'harmony' or 'discord'. 'Sin' as understood in the Judeo-Christian-Islamic sense does not exist in Sāṅkhya.

[18] There is no question of realizing pure-Spirit (Puruṣa/Self) less or more. We either know or don't! After Realization, there can be degrees to which attention is directed towards absorption, distraction, or habits, but once Nature and Spirit are truly understood, knowing remains.

10

# Transmission of Inquiry

एतत्पवित्रमग्र्यं मुनिरासुरयेऽनुकम्पया प्रददौ ।
आसुरिरपि पञ्चशिखाय तेन च बहुधा कृतं तन्त्रम् ॥ ७० ॥
etat pavitram agryam muniḥ āsuraye-anukaṃpayā ।
āsuriḥ api pañcaśikhāya tena ca bahudhā kṛtaṃ tantram ॥

– 70 –

*Great sage Kapila compassionately offered this sacred and highest wisdom to Āsuri, Āsuri taught it to his student Pañcaśikha,[19] he (Pañcaśikha) expanded and structured this wisdom in many ways.*

Having introduced Sāṅkhya philosophy, its origins, and tradition have also been provided: the great sage Kapila, who lived during ancient times, generously shared this wisdom with his student Āsuri. Later, sage Āsuri passed on the wisdom he received from his master to his student Pañcaśikha. Sage Pañcaśikha received this wisdom from his master Āsuri, expanding and structuring it so that he could share it with many of his students. Thus the Sāṅkhya School was born, in which masters shared their wisdom with their students.

This tradition was also followed by Sage Patañjali. He wrote a book called *Yoga Sutras* to assist students in their inquiry of the Self and not-Self. The underlying theory of Patañjali's *Yoga Sutras* is borrowed from the Sāṅkhya School, and physical and mental disciplines and practices are provided to assist students in

---

[19] In Theravadin Buddhism, Pañcaśikha was a king of a Gāndharva tribe (modern Afghanistan), and a divine musician who met Siddhartha Gotama, Śākyamūni, the Buddha. In Tibetan Buddhism, Pañcaśikha (पञ्चशिख) refers to "five crests" (5 dreadlocks) and is used to describe the Adi-Buddha (the primordial Buddha).

their inquiry of Nature and Spirit. Later in history, Sāṅkhya philosophers influenced the development of various forms of Buddhism and Zen.[20]

शिष्यपरम्परयाऽऽगतमीश्वरकृष्णेन चैतदार्याभिः ।
संक्षिप्तमार्यमतिना सम्यग्विज्ञाय सिद्धान्तम् ॥ ७१ ॥

śiṣya-paramparyā-agatam īśvarakṛṣṇena caitad āryābhiḥ ।
saṃkṣiptam āryamatinā saṃyak-vijñāya siddhāntam ॥

– 71 –

*This brief book is composed by Iśvarakṛṣṇa*
*in Āryā meter[21] with pure mind,*
*having received this wisdom by master-disciple tradition*
*and having understood it properly and thoroughly.*

Master Iśvarakṛṣṇa, who composed this work himself, is delivering an introduction to it. The work is written in Āryā poetic meter, without making it complicated or heavy. He received this great wisdom with a pure heart through the master-disciple tradition, studying and understanding it properly and thoroughly.

Unlike many other writers, master Iśvarakṛṣṇa ensures that, when composing this work, he did not write anything from his imagination or fantasy. This wisdom, which has been extensively studied and examined by many masters, wisdom which has endured for thousands of years and has been accepted by great minds throughout history, has been received and well understood by the writer Iśvarakṛṣṇa and is presented 'as-is', succinctly, and without any adulteration.

---

[20] Along with Vedānta, Vaishnavism, and Saivism, Sāṅkhya philosophy also inspired early Buddhist and Jain schools, some of which still teach forms of Sāṅkhya's inquiry and discernment,

[21] A verse in āryā meter is a unique poetic meter in Vedic and Jain poetry, originally taken from the gāthā meter of prākṛta, a more natural (or less refined) form of classical Sanskrit.

सप्तत्यां किल येऽर्थास्तेऽर्थाः कृत्स्नस्य षष्टितन्त्रस्य ।
आख्यायिकाविरहिताः परवादविवर्जिताश्चापि ॥ ७२ ॥

saptatyāṃ kila ye arthāḥ te arthāḥ kṛtsnasya ṣaṣṭitantrasya ।
ākhyāyikā-virahitāḥ paravāda-vivarjitāḥ cā api ॥

**– 72 –**

*All 60 topics that are discussed in the ancient Sāṅkhya scripture called Ṣaṣṭitantra[22] are discussed here too, excluding illustrative tales and omitting controversial dialogs.*

There are two approaches to teaching or studying philosophy: (1) the scriptural approach, known as *śāstra*, and (2) the topical approach, known as *prakaraṇa*. A scripture discusses the complete range of topics relating to their subject matter. It is a comprehensive approach to understanding every aspect of philosophy. The topical approach focuses on a select few of the most essential topics. It is a shortened method.

The writer is ensuring that this book does not fall into the category of a topical text (prakaraṇa-grantha), but rather into the category of scripture (śāstra-grantha) because it explains all of the 60 principles/topics discussed in another Sāṅkhya scripture known as the *Ṣaṣṭitantra*.

**Q**: If there is another book on Sāṅkhya philosophy, and that is a 'complete approach' book, then why study this book and not the *Ṣaṣṭitantra*?

**A**: That book is excessively large and complex to study because it thoroughly explains all other existing schools of thought, their viewpoints, and the negation of their views and thoughts, making the book heavy and complicated. Someone who is solely interested in removing suffering does not need to waste time understanding flawed schools of thought and putting forth

---

[22] *Ṣaṣṭitantra* (षष्टितन्त्र) = the name of a lost Sāṅkhya text, *"The 60 Ideas"*, written by a sage named Vṛṣagaṇa (वृषगण), whose family line dates back to a clan mentioned in the Ṛgveda (RV 9.97.7-9).

a lot of effort to refute those faulty notions that lead nowhere. It is a needless effort that will yield no worthwhile outcome. As a result, this straightforward book is presented. Unlike topical books (prakaraṇa-grantha), this book addresses all 60 principles and topics necessary to gain a complete understanding of Sāṅkhya philosophy.

What are those 60 ideas?[23]

## 10 Fundamental Principles for Understanding Nature and Spirit

1. Passage 14: **Establishment of Primordial Nature** (By Logic)
2. Passage 15: **The Oneness of Nature** (There is only One Nature)
3. Passage 11: **Usefulness of Nature** (Experiences, Liberation, Creation)
4. Passage 11: **Differentiation between Nature and Spirit**
5. Passage 17: **Nature is an 'Object of Experience' in Service of Spirit**
6. Passage 18: **Multiplicity of Intellects and Spirits**
7. Passage 20: **Separation of Spirit from Nature = Liberation**
8. Passage 21: **Confusion between Spirit and Nature = Bondage**
9. Passage 39: **Existence of Gross and Subtle Bodies**
10. Passage 19: **Inactiveness of Spirit** (neither doer nor controller)

[23] The 60 Ideas are presented in a slightly different order here to simplify oral instruction.

## 50 Additional Topics
## Concerning Spiritual Attainments, Ignorance, and Error

### Passage 47: *5 Types of Abstraction*

11. **Ignorance** as lack of discernment between Nature and Spirit
12. **Pride** as a result of confusing not-Self with the true-Self
13. **Attachment** to seeking fulfillment through materialism
14. **Aversion** to limitations when seeking fulfillment
15. **Fear** of death, non-existence, and losing objects of attachment

### Passage 50: *9 Types of Contentments*

16. **Content with Scientific Knowledge** vs. Self-knowledge
17. **Content with Self-image** and appearance vs. Self-knowledge
18. **Content with Waiting** for spontaneous awakening vs. Self-knowledge
19. **Content with Luck** as causal to spiritual awakening vs. Self-knowledge

20. – 24. **Content with Withdrawal** of the 5 senses vs. Self-knowledge

### Passage 49: *28 Types of Instrumental Disabilities*

25. – 29. **Disability of the 5 Senses** (eyes, ears, nose, skin, mouth)

30. – 34. **Disability of the 5 Organs** (speech, hands, feet, genitals, anus)

35. **Disability of Mental Health** (3-fold mind/intellect, ego, mind)

36. – 44. **Defects of 9 Contentments** (to ignore seeking Self-knowledge)

45. – 52. **Defects of 8 Attainments** (abstraction, contentment, disability)

### Passage 51: *8 types of Attainments*

53. **Reasoning** to understand the Self (Spirit) and not-Self (Nature)
54. **Listening** to teachers
55. **Study** of spiritual teachings and texts

56. – 58. **Prevention** of 3-Fold Suffering (Inner / Outer / Extraordinary)

59. **Good Company** in the form of teachers, classmates, and friends
60. **Purity**, free of conflict, doubt, misapprehension, and Self-ignorance

### *Points for Reflection*

- Apart from historical context,[24] Chapter 10 provides a neat overview of the 60 principles and topics taught in Sāṅkhya philosophy.
- **The 10 Fundamental Principles**:[25] These assertions make up the foundation of Sāṅkhya philosophy. These alone are enough to lead the student to intellectual understanding and to liberating knowledge. They direct the student to a clear understanding of Nature and Spirit.
- **The 50 Additional Topics**:[26] These negations explain why such deep and binding ignorance and error seem to persist. These assist us in our logical inquiry by helping to clarify the factors that keep us feeling bound to Nature, and point out their benefits, weaknesses, and uses. They direct the student to a clear understanding of just why Nature alone, without the knowledge of Spirit, is binding and inadequate to provide Liberation.
- **The 8 types of attainments**:[27] These are useful to help prepare and purify us on the path towards Realization and Liberation, but they also can be binding as well. They are presented in the context of addressing their potential for binding influence.

---

[24] Chapter 10, passages 71 and 72 are believed by some scholars to be a later addition to the original text.

[25] The order that these are taught can vary from teacher to teacher, school to school.

[26] The order that these are taught can also vary. In some cases, *Contentments* are discussed before the *Disabilities* as presented on page 101.

[27] These are sometimes taught in the positive as spiritual disciplines and attainments. In this text however, they are distinctly highlighted as causes of continuing bondage.

# Conclusion: Yoga & Spirituality Today

When the word *'Yoga'* is mentioned nowadays, people think of a set of physical practices that are beneficial to flexibility, physical health, and overall well-being. Unfortunately, many people who call themselves Yoga teachers and instructors know very little about what the term *'Yoga'* actually means.

Many (but not all) people who claim to be experts in Yoga philosophy (Sāṅkhya) know little to nothing about Yoga's origins, or why this school of yogic practices was formed. Numerous beliefs and superstitions have also developed within this school. In addition, many fake gurus exist, who take advantage of people by purporting to have supernatural powers from yogic practices while knowing nothing about what authentic Yoga is.

Yoga has recently gained popularity all around the world. There are numerous Yoga instructors and practitioners in many nations, but the vast majority of them overlook the essence of Yoga – Divine Union. In the Katha Upanishad, there is a fantastic phrase that refers to these types of teachers and their followers: *"the blind leading the blind.* (अन्धेन नियमाना यथा अन्धाः ।)"

A true Yoga practitioner must understand what Yoga is and why this school was created in the first place. Who were the philosophers who founded this school, and what exactly did they intend to share with the rest of the world?

Many individuals confuse physical activities with spirituality; some believe that practicing some āsana and breathing exercises makes them spiritual and superior to others; some like to blame others for their eating choices, claiming to know what true spirituality is. It is quite unfortunate to see people engaging in all manner of nonsense in the name of spirituality.

In Rishikesh, where I live, hundreds of commercial Yoga training centers can be found. Rishikesh is a small town in the Indian Himalayas that serves as a hub for the study of Yoga and Vedānta. Here reside yogis and brahmacāris who are familiar with Sāṅkhya and the *Yoga Sutras* of Patañjali. Personally, I haven't found a single individual teaching at the commercial Yoga centers who has formally studied Yoga philosophy – Sāṅkhya – or has any in-depth knowledge of it. In most situations, Yoga has become a means of making money and gaining followers. False teachers just pretend to know about Yoga while focusing on physical health benefits and the appearance of being spiritual.

Many people who profess to understand Yoga philosophy are only familiar with Sāṅkhya from Patañjali's book, the *Yoga Sutras*. This text borrows Kapila's Sāṅkhya philosophy but expands its principles very little. If we ask them (current commercial Yoga teachers) what Sāṅkhya truly is, most have little to no idea. Furthermore, when you ask them about the real purpose of the *Yoga Sutras*, they also miss the mark. Very few will reply, "divine-union", by which we actually mean "Yoga".

Even the vast majority of 'advanced Yoga teacher training' courses barely cover the *Yoga Sutras*, and none that I am personally aware of incorporates the *Sāṅkhyakārikā* as a core component of the program. There are well-respected Yoga teachers who, unfortunately, know very little about the subject. False teachers, those who teach Yoga without knowing its spiritual basis, are indeed the *"blind leading the blind"*.

How are physical activities spiritual? If this is the case, why aren't all physical activities spiritual? Gymnastics or calisthenics, in my opinion, can have an equivalent or much better effect on strength, flexibility, and balance than any āsana practice. The spiritual foundation must be there to differentiate Yoga.

People believe that wearing white clothes, wearing rosaries and crystals around their necks, and being vegetarian or vegan make them spiritual. Those; who are confused in this manner live their lives in complete ignorance or worse, grow arrogant and even competitive with their spirituality, unknowingly developing a spiritual ego. This is what it means to be spiritually ignorant! The knowledge gained through Sāṅkhya is a remedy to this.

Let us try to understand fully what Yoga or spirituality actually means. The word *'Yoga'* is derived from the Sanskrit root *yujir* (युजिर्), which means *'joining'* or *'attainment'*. Let us look into a few classical definitions of the term *'Yoga'*:

योगः कर्मसु कौशलम्

Yoga is skillfulness in action.

— *Bhagavad-Gītā*

Master Kṛṣṇa explains how to transcend the suffering caused by emotional fluctuations; the term 'skillfulness' here refers to not being emotionally impacted by the outcome of any activity. When a yogi acts with full engagement and dedication, yet without longing for its result, it leads to inner satisfaction, and thus the yogi overcomes frustration.

समत्वं योग उच्यते

Yoga is equanimity.

— *Bhagavad-Gītā*

Nature (Prakṛti) and its collective product have three qualities: sāttva, rājas, and tamas, whereas Spirit (Puruṣa) is free from any qualities. Yoga is the equanimity attained through this realization of Self (Spirit) and not-Self (Nature). Yogis realize the distinction between Self and not-Self. All actions, reactions, changes, and fluctuations are a product of Nature, not Spirit, and hence yogis overcome all afflictions, frustrations, and suffering and realize 'equanimity'.

योगः चित्तवृत्ति निरोधः

Yoga is cessation of mental afflictions.

— *Yoga Sutras of Patañjali*

Yoga, according to Sāṅkhya, is the understanding of Spirit and Nature. Yoga, according to certain other philosophers, is the realization of the supreme-Self. Kapila is Sāṅkhya philosophy's great grandmaster. True freedom, according to Kapila, is only possible by having a correct comprehension of Self (Spirit) and not-Self (Nature). Later in history, master Patañjali taught several disciplines and practices that were highly beneficial in preparing for the realization of Spirit and Nature. True spirituality is a correct understanding of Spirit – Spirit that is unaffected by Nature and its qualities and effects. Know that the body-mind organism is a part of Nature, ever-changing, yet mistaken for Self due to ignorance and error. Spirit, the true-Self, is ever free of all phenomena.

# Afterword

*by Silvia Beitia Fernandez*

It was my friend and Advaita Vedānta teacher J. Erik LaPort who mentioned Sāṅkhya to me for the first time and the influence of this dualistic philosophy had on what later became the Yoga Sutras of Patañjali. He then sent me a copy and at first glance, I thought it was quite a difficult text to read and comprehend, so I told him my thoughts on it. Little did I know that that innocent comment would then turn into this beautiful translation and commentary by Suraj, and we discussed a workshop on the subject.

My first Yoga experience was in Thailand with a Californian man and his Italian wife, nestled in a small town bordering Laos. Over the years and especially after I became a teacher, I realized how lucky I was that that was my first taste of Yoga. They were teaching an intensive beginner's course with a set āsana sequence, prāṇāyāma, meditation, and talks about philosophy and anatomy of Yoga. Soon enough, I realized that that wasn't the case for most people attending classes in the western world. After going to a few classes and observing there was no mention of the spiritual side of the Yoga practice or even time to pause in the posture and breath, I stopped attending and continued my practice as I was first taught. Only when I moved to Koh Tao, my home of 14 years now, I started to attend Shambhala, the Yoga school where I have been now teaching for eleven years.[28]

After a class, it dawned on me that I wanted to share this ancient practice and became a teacher. It was only after Kester, owner of Shambhala and a true tāntrika at heart, introduced me to Clive Sheridan, his teacher, I started to understand what he calls *"enquiring into the matters of heart and mind"*. This was the beginning of my spiritual journey. My understanding matured when I

---

[28] https://www.shambhalayogakohtao.com/

met Erik and noticed there was something in me that wanted to dive deeper into the intellectual aspect of Yoga, that of self-enquiry, and I became one of his students of Advaita Vedanta amongst other spiritual traditions.

As a Yoga teacher, I couldn't fail to notice the parallels between Sāṅkhya and the Yoga Sutras. It seems that Patañjali built the sutras on Sāṅkhya's notions of Puruṣa (Spirit) and Prakṛti (Matter), with Sāṅkhya being the theory and Yoga the practice, hence the importance of this ancient text if we want to understand the origins of Yoga and its spiritual foundation. Ultimately, these teachings are not only for people interested in deepening their Yoga practice but anyone who wants to gain a deeper understanding of who we really are, our true nature and everything around us. By examining the transient nature of the material world, we can transcend our conditioned minds and connect with Consciousness, from which everything arises.

Sāṅkhya presents us with a clear model to discern material Nature (Prakṛti) from Spirit (Puruṣa). It starts with why are we enquiring on the first place, the root cause being suffering and its removal taking us into knowledge of the Self by understanding first the not-Self through a comprehensive model that has 25 elements, 24 being part of Nature (not-Self) and 1 element, Spirit (true-Self). The yogic model adds one more element (God, Īśvara). It then proceeds to explain in detail the 24 elements that comprise Nature as well as how to discriminate or discern by valid means of knowledge, reasoning into the nature of Spirit leading us to *Yoga* or *Union*.

Suraj's commentary enumerates the hindrances, the obstacles to realizing our true nature (3-fold obstructions), and how to counteract with the 8-fold attainments. To finish with we are guided to how to attain spiritual Freedom by realizing that we are not the body-mind organism, not anything that has qualities, nor anything that can be perceived or subject to change.

Lastly, I would like to add that Yoga without its spiritual foundation is merely gymnastics, which I find is the biggest problem nowadays with Yoga around the world. Yoga today is being portrayed as merely just another physical discipline without considering the most essential aspect of the practice – *UNION* – the very meaning of the word *YOGA*, uniting the personal with the universal through transcending mind and body and finally realizing our Divine nature. The physical aspect of the practice should be paired with transcendent knowledge and this is where Sāṅkhya comes into play.

As we experience a rapid development of technology and science, people seem to be more attached than ever to their physical attributes and abilities, achievements, money and power. Meanwhile, mental illness appears to be on the rise, people seem lonelier and more disconnected from inner Truth than ever. This is one more reason why we should preserve and teach this ancient philosophy, to help us gain understanding of who (or what) we really are, and enjoy this cosmic play we call life with joy, compassion, and equanimity.

# Appendix A

## Bhāgavata Purāṇa

(Book 3, Ch. 27 – The Sāṅkhya Philosophy: Puruṣa and Prakṛti)

***Kapila said to his mother Devahūti:***

1. Though Spirit (Puruṣa) resides in the body (which is a product of Nature), it is not affected by the qualities (guṇas), of Nature (such as pleasure, pain, etc.), just as the Sun (in the sky) reflected in the water (remains unaffected by the water). For Spirit is devoid of qualities (guṇas), hence its freedom from action and changelessness thereby.
2. When this person is attached to the qualities of Nature, it becomes deluded by ego and regards itself as the doer (through arrogation).
3. Due to that (ego), it loses its independence and blessed state. By the force of the (detrimental) effects of actions due to the association with Nature, it gets involved in cycles of suffering (saṃsāra) in some form of existence, good, bad, or a combination.
4. (Spirit as non-doer), the real bondage of actions does not exist. Nevertheless, the cycle of suffering does not cease so long as the person is worrying over the (sense-) objects, like how one experiences misfortunes in a dream (even though the dream is unreal).
5. Therefore, the mind that is attached to the terrific path of sensual enjoyment should be gradually brought under control through the path of devotion and intense dispassion (towards materialism).
6. – 11. Whoever practices meditation by the path of Yoga characterized by stages like yama, niyama, etc. (i.e., Patañjali's 8-limbs of Yoga), is full of trust in me by real, sincere love for me, and by listening to stories about me, looks upon all beings as equal, renouncing all attachment and company; hates nobody, practices celibacy, and observes silence, follows their own duties which are powerful on account of offering them to God, that sage who is satisfied with whatever they get by chance, is moderate in eating, resorts to solitude, is serene and friendly

to all and self-controlled, does not entertain false attachment (like 'me' and 'mine') to the body and its dependents or property, has the knowledge whereby one can realize the truth about Nature (Prakṛti/not-Self) and Spirit (Puruṣa/true-Self), has superseded the stages like wakefulness, sleep, etc., and hence has ceased to see other things except God. The Self-seer sage realizes his Soul (Atman) by his Self just as one sees the Sun (in the sky) by the eye which is also a modified Sun, (such a sage) realizes that nondual Absolute (Brahman) which is completely distinct and free from the subtle-body and which appears as real in unrealities like the ego which is the friend, i.e. the basis of Primordial Cause; which is like a witness to the unreal and which is woven fully into all causes and effects.

12. – 14. As the reflected sun is understood by its reflection on the (mirror on the) wall, and the sun in the sky (which is up) is understood by looking at its reflection in the water (looking down), thus the 3-fold ego is understood by its association with the body, mind, and senses, then the true-Self can be realized by the analysis of ego that is the fourth (Turīya) and free of all the conditioning of the 3-fold ego, which is present even in deep-sleep where the conditioning of body-mind-senses are not functioning.

15. In that state, when the ego is dormant (lit. lost), the Seer (the person), though himself is not lost, wrongly thinks that he is lost, like a man stricken with grief at the loss of his fortune, feels (about himself).

16. In this way, having thoroughly thought over (this distinctness of the Self), the Self is realized, which is the basis and the illuminator of all the objects (of Awareness) including ego.

***Devahūti replied:***

17. Brahman, as both (Nature and Spirit) are interdependent and eternal, Nature never leaves the Spirit.

18. Just as the existence of smell and the earth or of taste and water cannot be mutually separate, Nature and Spirit cannot be logically discontinuous (i.e. cannot exist independently).

19. How can there be freedom from Nature (saṃsāra cycle of suffering) when the qualities (3 guṇas) of Nature are in existence. These qualities form bondage of actions to Spirit, which is inactive.

20. Sometimes the terrible fear (of the cycle of suffering) may seem withdrawn by careful reflection about the Principles (of Sāṅkhya). However, as its cause is not destroyed, the fear appears again.

21. – 23. By performance of one's duties without any desire for its fruit, by pure mind, and by devotion intensified by hearing the stories about reality for a long period, by knowledge which has comprehended the reality, by a very strong aversion to the world, by Yoga accompanied with asceticism, and by intense concentration on the Self, Nature, being consumed day and night, gradually disappears in this very birth like the piece of firewood, the source of fire, (is burnt away by the fire).

24. Nature having been abandoned after enjoying her, and whose negative effects are always seen, does not bear anything inauspicious to the supreme Self established in its magnificence.

25. Just as a dream presents a great many of tragedies to someone who is not awakened (but is dreaming), but the same (dream) is not capable of deluding them when they are awake.

26. Similarly, Nature never causes any harm to one who has realized the Truth, who has set their heart upon Truth, and who is delighted in realizing the Self.

27. When a sage is delighted in the Self, and after going through many births is unattached and free from everything including the highest heaven.

28. – 29. (and being) devoted has realized the true Self, by grace, easily realizes the essential state, as distinct from the physical body – a state of final beatitude called Unity-absolute (kaivalya). The wise one, who has resolved all doubts by realization of the Self, goes by grace to the state attained after transcending the subtle body and from which state there is no relapse.

***Kapila responded:***

30. Oh Mother, when the mind of the liberated sage is unattached to the miraculous powers born of Yoga and obtained through yogic practice, then only is realized the ultimate state – a state where even death is powerless.

# Appendix B

## Sāṅkhya Yoga in the Bhagavad-gītā

(Chapter 2)

The 2nd chapter of the Bhagavad-gītā is named *"Sāṅkhya Yoga"*. passages 1 thru 10 concern disturbed emotional and mental states. Passages 11 thru 39 present the basic teaching of Sāṅkhya Yoga, the *'Yoga of Reasoning'*. Passages 40 thru 72 address the practical application of Sāṅkhya Yoga, the practice called Buddhi-Karma Yoga, the *'Yoga of Intelligent Actions'*. Buddhi-Karma Yoga can be summarized by the equation: right attitude + right behavior = Buddhi-Karma Yoga, by which all actions are seen as a form of reverence for the divinity that underlies all existence.

Seven aspects of spirituality are touched upon in the 2nd Chapter of the Gītā:

1. ***Self-knowledge***: differentiating Self and not-Self, understanding Self
2. ***Discernment***: differentiating Real and unreal, understanding Reality
3. ***Detachment***: worldly engagement free of attachment to outcomes
4. ***Discipline***: focus on emotion-free disciplined fulfillment of duties
5. ***Renunciation of Action***: selfless action dedicated to a higher purpose
6. ***Inquiry***: philosophical insights and inquiry to attain spiritual wisdom
7. ***Path to Liberation***: understanding interconnectedness and the Self

Below are a selection of passages from chapter 2 of the Gītā that conveys the feel and flavor of Sāṅkhya as expressed by Veda Vyāsa:

### *The Yoga of Reasoning (Sāṅkhya Yoga)*

> BG 2.14: The relationship between the senses and the sense-objects give birth to experiences such as favorable and unfavorable experiences. These experiences are impermanent and transient. Therefore, you can only endure them.

BG 2.15: A person who is not bothered by the pairs of opposites and retains his equanimity, such a person realizes Freedom.

BG 2.19: A person who thinks that the Self is an object of any action or the doer of any action, does not understand. It cannot kill or be killed.

BG 2.20: It is not born nor will it die. It is not limited by past, present, or future. It is without origin or birth. It is permanent, changeless, and ageless. It does not perish with the destruction of a body.

BG 2.21: Understand the Self as changeless, eternal, birthless, and partless or indestructible.

BG 2.29: Some see the Self as a wonder, talk about it as a wonder. Some others listen to it as a wonder and some others don't understand even after listening about it.

BG 2.39: Now you listen to this wisdom of Sāṅkhya. After realizing it [the wisdom therein], you will be free from all suffering.

### *The Yoga of Intelligent Actions (Buddhi-Karma Yoga)*

BG 2.41: A realized mind is one that is established on the one reality. A confused mind is one that is scattered in many directions.

BG 2.45: Knowledge (Vedas) deals with interplay of the three qualities (3 guṇas; tamās, rājas, sāttva); worldly enjoyments and the means of attaining such enjoyments. Be indifferent to these enjoyments and their means, rising above duality such as pleasure and pain etc., established in the eternal Self, absolutely unconcerned about fulfilling desires and preserving what has already been attained, and retain self-control.

BG 2.47: One has the right to perform their expected duty, but not the right to the fruits of action. One should not consider oneself as the doer of the action, nor should one attach oneself to inaction.

BG 2.50: The wise renounce their identifications with both good and bad deeds. (The result is) to overcome all suffering, therefore one must strive for Sāṅkhya Yoga to attain equanimity. Buddhi-Karma Yoga is an intelligent perspective.

BG 2.53: When the realized intelligence becomes stable in the understanding of the Supreme through long-term contemplation, it is the culmination of Sāṅkhya Yoga.

BG 2.55b: One who is self-established through Self-realization (the supreme-Self) is a *'sage of steady wisdom'*.[29]

BG 2.65: A person who realizes the true nature of Self overcomes all suffering. A person of pleasant mind finds it easy to realize the Self.

BG 2.71: A person who renounces all desires through dispassion and moves without identification and ego, such a person realizes supreme peace.

BG 2.72: This is the state of supreme understanding; having realized it, one is no longer self-deceived.

[29] sthitaprajña = firm in judgement and wisdom; contented; calm

# Appendix C

## Avadhūtaka Upaniṣad

(Laghu – Minor Section)

This is the 8-Limbed Yoga: (1) control, (2) discipline, (3) posture, (4) breath control, (5) withdrawal, (6) yogic concentration, (7) meditation, (8) union.

*Detachment from the body and the senses* is called ***self-control*** by the wise.

*Constant attachment to the highest Truth* is said to be ***purifying discipline.***

*Indifference toward all things* is the foremost ***posture control.***

*The conviction that this whole world is illusory* constitutes ***breath control.***

When *the mind is focused within itself, that* is the best ***sense-withdrawal.***

*Maintaining the steadfastness of mind*, they consider being ***concentration.***

The thought *"I am just pure-Consciousness"* is said to be ***meditation.***

The total oblivion of meditation is termed ***absorption / bliss of union.***

Having thus purified the instruments, the yogi with the mind free of desires comes to rest in the Self, just as a fire when its fuel is spent.

When there is nothing to be grasped, the yogi, free of mind and breath and endowed with steadfast knowledge, becomes dissolved in the pure and supreme reality, like a lump of salt dissolved in water.

The yogi has torn to pieces the web of delusion, seeing everything as if it were a dream. By the yogi's very nature, supremely unwavering, the yogi goes about (serene) as if in deep sleep. Entering the state of cessation *(nirvāṇa),* the yogi attains absolute union *(kaivalya; eternal happiness and freedom).*

The yogi, indeed, realizes absolute union, and thus is *'one who knows'*.

That is the secret teaching.

# About the Author

Suraj Santosh Sarode (Āśutoṣa) left home in Maharashtra as a teenager traveling to Alandi to pursue a life as a spiritual renunciate studying and living on alms. After a few years, he made his way to Varanasi, one of the world's oldest continuously inhabited cities, located on the banks of the Ganges in the heart of the Gangetic plain. For millennia, Varanasi has been a center for spiritual study, and it was here that Suraj began Sanskrit studies in earnest while training as a priest and temple cook. Suraj's interests later led him to Haridwar, another center of spirituality and gateway to the Himalayas. At Haridwar, Suraj continued in service again as a priest for a time before entering into formal study of Sanskrit, Logic, and Vedanta.

Ultimately, his calling led him to Arsha Vidya Institute for Sanskrit and Vedanta (commonly known as Dayananda Ashram) in Rishikesh, where he lived and studied full-time as a resident student-initiate for several years. Life at Arsha Vidya brought Suraj into contact with many earnest and devoted western students of spiritual philosophy. Suraj was affectionately known as the *'spiritual surgeon'* or *'spiritual technician'* for his razor-sharp ability to spot errors and clear up misunderstandings in Vedantic doctrine. Suraj has assisted many western seekers in clarifying the finer points of spiritual philosophy and improving their written and spoken Sanskrit.

Suraj's 14-year initiatic process was rigorous and comprehensive, and he still refers to himself as a *'student of Vedānta'*. He is an inner-renunciate (āntara saṃnyāsin; आन्तर संन्यासिन्) who lives a quiet life of study, nonviolence, detachment, and clarity amid a society and a world that is anything but.

ashutoshshivah@gmail.com

www.ingramcontent.com/pod-product-compliance
Lightning Source LLC
Chambersburg PA
CBHW070717130626
46553CB00005B/2023
*9798988062257*